KT-133-320

Contents

Arthur Miller

Chronology of professionally produced plays

	First US production	First UK production
The Man Who Had All the Luck	23.1.44	28.4.60
All My Sons	29.1.47	11.5.48
Death of a Salesman	10.2.49	28.7.49
An Enemy of the People (adapted from Ibsen)	28.12.50	
The Crucible	22.1.53	9.11.54
A Memory of Two Mondays	29.9.55	29.9.58
A View from the Bridge (one-act version)	29.9.55	
(two-act version)	28.1.65	11.10.56
After the Fall	23.1.64	31.10.67
The Price	7.2.68	4.3.69
The Creation of the World and Other Business	30.11.72	17.8.74
Up from Paradise (musical)	23.4.74	
The Archbishop's Ceiling	30.4.77	1.4.85
The American Clock	24.5.80	18.4.83
Two-Way Mirror	11.82	
Playing for Time (adapted from his screenplay)	22.9.85	
Danger: Memory!	1.87	6.4.88
The Golden Years	(world première)	6.11.87
The Ride Down Mount Morgan	(world première)	23.10.91
The Last Yankee	5.1.93	21.1.93
Broken Glass	9.3.94	4.8.94

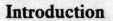

Introduction

About Theatre Language

I

When I began writing plays in the late thirties, something called realism was the undisputed reigning style in the American commercial theatre – which was just about all the theatre there was in this country. The same was more or less the case in Britain. Theatre then could still be thought of as, if not a mass then at least a popular art, although one knew – long before television – that something of its common appeal had gone out of it, and a lot of its twenties glamour, too. One blamed the movies, which had stolen so much of the audience and thus theatre's old power as a cultural influence.

Notwithstanding the obvious fact that the audience was predominantly middle class, we continued to imagine that we were making plays for an audience made up of a representative variety of the city and even the country, people of many different educational and cultural levels. If this was never really true there was certainly no thought of appealing to a clique of college graduates or to academics and their standards. A *New York Times* critic like George S. Kaufman had both feet in show business and became the most popular writer of comedies of the period, while Brooks Atkinson may have had one eye on Aristotle but understood that his readers were Americans impatient with any theatrical enterprise that required either education or patience. Still, outside New York there were at least the remains of the twenties' touring wheel, theatres in many smaller cities regularly attended by quite ordinary citizens eager for last year's Broadway hits, albeit with replacement casts. In New York, with a ticket price of fifty-five cents to four dollars and forty cents, one somehow took for granted that a professor might be sitting next to a housewife, a priest beside a skilled worker perhaps, a grammar school teacher, a small or large business executive beside a student. True or not, this conception of the demotic audience influenced the writing of plays directed at the commonsensical experience of everyday people. Missing were black or Asian or Hispanic faces, of course, but they were beyond the consciousness of the prevailing culture. As for production costs, even into the forties they were relatively within reason; plays like *All My Sons* or *Death of a Salesman*, for example, cost between twenty and forty thousand to produce, a budget small enough to be raised among half a dozen modest contributors who might lose all with some embarrassment but reasonably little pain, or make a killing.

Radicals – people like myself, trying to convince ourselves that we were carrying on the age-old tradition of theatre as a civic art rather than a purely commercial one, were in a conflict; to attract even the fitful interest of a Broadway producer, and subsequently to engage the audience, we had to bow to realism, even if it was the poetic forms that we really admired or at least wished to explore. An Expressionist like the German, Ernst Toller, for example, would not have been read past his sixth page by a Broadway producer or a London one for that matter. There is not one playwright among what one thinks of as the important ones of the age who was – or is now – welcome in the commercial theatre. Not Chekhov, not Ibsen, not Hauptmann, not Pirandello, Strindberg, Turgenev – not even Shaw. To so much as perform a Beckett play like *Godot* in the general proximity of Broadway one has to have a cast of movie stars for a very short run, as was done a little while back at Lincoln

Center, and things were probably a bit worse half a century ago. One need only read O'Neill's letters of complaint at the 'showshop' of Broadway and the narrow compass of the American theatre audience's imagination – or in Britain, Shaw's ridiculing his countrymen's provincialism – to understand the problem; for some mysterious reason the Anglo-Saxon culture regarded theatre as an entertainment first and last, an art of escape with none of the Continental or Russian involvement with its moral or philosophical opportunities or obligations. Very occasionally in America there was an *Adding Machine* by the young Elmer Rice, but such a break-out from conventional realism was rare enough to be brought up in conversation for years after, like a calf born with five legs. The English language theatre was pridefully commercial, a profit-making enterprise which wed it to a form whose surfaces of familiar reality would be universally recognized. Captain Shotover's outcry, 'I like to know where I am!' could have been sewn to the flag of this theatre. Unless it were a musical; they alone had the happy licence to stretch reality, at least to some extent. But for straight plays even satire was too strange to prosper; George Kaufman defined satire as what closes on Saturday night.

The point here is that what we think of as 'straight realism' was tiresome half a century ago, and indeed longer than that, but it was unquestioned as a reflection of life by the audiences and almost all the reviewers. At the same time it should be remembered that one or another of realism's multiplicity of variants has re-emerged at various moments to express very capably the essence of an era. At a time when 'experimental' is all the virtue a play needs in order to gain serious consideration, it is not a bad idea to confess that extraordinarily few such researches have achieved any kind of enduring life. It is not quite enough to know how to escape; one has also to think of arriving somewhere.

In the thirties, probably the single exception – at least that I was aware of – to realism's domination was the WPA's *Living Newspaper*, the one formal innovation of American theatre. An epic in more or less presentational form, written like movies by groups of writers rather than individually, it dealt in an overtly exuberant spirit with social issues like public ownership of electrical power, labour unions, agriculture, and medicine, and was extremely popular. But significantly, the WPA was government subsidized, using unemployed actors, designers, technicians, and did not need to make a profit, so a show could call upon large casts and elaborate scenery and production elements. And the ticket was low-priced. It could send Orson Welles, for example, into Harlem storefronts with a big cast playing *Doctor Faustus*, charging a quarter a seat. But theatre-for-profit was hardly affected by what might be called this epic-populist approach – it was simply too expensive to produce.

I mention these mundane things because they profoundly affect style in the theatre which, like politics, is always the art of the possible.

There were at least a dozen playwrights regularly feeding the commercial theatre in those years before World War Two, and all but perhaps Odets and Hellman would have pridefully declared that their sole purpose was to entertain. Those playwrights were sophisticated and no doubt knew all about the Continental theatre tradition and its aspiring to the philosophical condition, something like that of the Greeks or in a different way the Elizabethans. The Theatre Guild, for one, had been started in the twenties in part to bring that kind of theatre to America, the theatre of Pirandello, Schnitzler, Ibsen, Strindberg, and so on.

In the thirties, one American styled himself a political revolutionary, and that was Clifford Odets. O'Neill, of course, had been the aesthetic rebel but his socialism was private rather than informing his plays, although *The Hairy Ape* is surely an anti-capitalist work. It was his formal experiments and tragic mood that set him apart. O'Neill was a totally isolated phenomenon in the Broadway theatre as a maker and user of new and old theatrical forms.

Odets, on the other hand, while describing himself as 'a man of the Left', was, with the possible exception of his first play, *Waiting For Lefty*, no innovator where form was concerned. He attempted a poetic realism but it was still trying to represent real people in actual social relationships. And this was perhaps inevitable given his actor's temperament as well as his Marxist commitment; he had the revolutionary's eye on the great public, on the reconstitution of power once a failed capitalism had been brought down – for such was the Marxist and non-Marxist Left position on the proper moral obligation of the artist. But by temperament he was a poet seeking words that would lift him into a take-off, regardless of his realist political commitments.

O'Neill, on the other hand, was not the revolutionary but the rebel with a despairing anarchism in his heart. If he glimpsed any salvation, it was not to arrive in a more benign reconstitution of political power but in the tragic cleansing of the life-lie which is permanently ensconced in the human condition. Since he took no responsibility in theory for a new and better polity to take the place of the corrupted present one, he was free to explore all sorts of theatrical means by which to set forth the situation of the damned. Moreover, if O'Neill wanted his plays to register, and he surely did, they need not be popular to justify his having written them, for he was hunting the sounding whale of ultimate meaning, and he expected to suffer for it; oppositely, a critical or box-office failure for Odets meant rejection of a very personal kind, a spit in the eye by an ungrateful, self-satisfied bourgeois society. A failed play for Odets was a denial of what he was owed, for he was chasing the public no differently than his bourgeois non-revolutionary contemporaries, fickle as the public always is. O'Neill could say, as he did, that he was not interested in relations between men, but between Man and God. For America, in his view, was damned and if there were a few individuals who behaved justly and well it was not because they belonged to a particular social class or held a generous or selfish political viewpoint, but by virtue of a grace whose source is beyond definition.

II

The realism of Broadway – and Shaftesbury Avenue and the Boulevard theatre of France – was detested by the would-be poetic dramatists of my generation, just as it had always been since it came into vogue in the nineteenth century. What did this realism really come down to? A play representing real rather than symbolic or metaphysical persons and situations, its main virtue verisimilitude, with no revolutionary implications for society or even a symbolic statement of some general truth. Quite simply, conventional realism was conventional because it implicitly supported the conventions of society, but it could just as easily do something quite different, or so it seemed to me. Nevertheless, we thought it the perfect style for an unchallenging, simple-minded linear middle-class conformist view of life. What I found confusing at the time, however, was that not so very long before the name 'realism' had been applied to the revolutionary style of playwrights like Ibsen, Chekhov and quite frequently Strindberg, writers whose whole thrust was in opposition to the bourgeois status quo and the hypocrisies on which it stood, or in Chekhov's case the futilities of the Czarist system.

My own first playwriting attempt was purely mimetic, a realistic play about my own family. It won me some prizes and productions, but interestingly, I turned at once to a stylized treatment of life in a gigantic prison – modelled on Jackson State Penitentiary in Michigan, near Ann Arbor where I was in school, the largest prison in the United States, which I had visited over weekends with a friend who was its lone psychologist. The theme of that play was that prisons existed to make desperate working men insane. There was a chorus of sane prisoners chanting from a high overpass above the stage, and a counter-chorus of the insane trying to draw the other into their ranks. It was inevitable that I had to confront the problem of dramatic language, for it was impossible to engage so vast a human disaster with speech born in a warm kitchen. I gradually came to wonder if the essential pressure toward poetic dramatic language – if not toward stylization itself – came from the inclusion of society as a major element in the play's story or vision. Manifestly, prose realism was the language of the individual and of private life, poetry the language of man in crowds, in society. Put another way, prose is the language of family relations; it is the inclusion of the larger world beyond that naturally opens a play to the poetic.

But I wanted to succeed, I wanted to engage and grip an audience. Minds might be illuminated by speeches thrown at them but it was by being moved that one was changed. And so the problem was that our audiences were trained, as it were, in a pallid realism and were turned off by stylistic novelty, by 'art'. How to find a style which would at one and the same time deeply engage an American audience which insisted on a recognizable reality of characters, locales and themes, while opening the stage to considerations of public morality and the mythic social fates – in short, the invisible?

Of course this was not my preoccupation alone. I doubt

there was ever a time when so much discussion went on about form and style. T.S. Eliot was writing his verse plays, and Auden and Isherwood theirs, the poetic mimesis of Sean O'Casey was most popular, and W.B. Yeats' dialogue was studied if not very often produced. The impulse to poetry reached into the ex-newspaperman and realistic writer Maxwell Anderson, whose attempts to imitate Elizabethan prosody with contemporary characters and social themes were widely celebrated, as curios by some, as moving experiences by others.

To be just to Odets – it was he who challenged the Broadway theatre's addiction to verisimilitude by his idiosyncratic dialogue, and he was surely the first American playwright to be celebrated – and more wildly and lavishly than any other before him – for his writing style. For younger writers such as myself, Odets for a couple of years was the trailblazer; he was bringing the suffering of the Great Depression onto the Broadway stage and making them listen. If he had not solved the problem of a contemporary American style he had dared invent an often wildly stylized stage speech. But I suppose that since his characters lacked elegance or strangeness but were the very exemplars of realistic theatre, Odets was called a realist – indeed, a kind of reporter, no less, of Jewish life in the Bronx. I may not have lived in the Bronx but the speech of Brooklyn Jews certainly had no resemblance to Odets' people.

Carp (in *Golden Boy*): 'I'm super-disgusted with you!' 'A man hits his wife and it's the first step to fascism!' 'Look in the papers! On every side the clouds of war!' 'Ask yourself a pertinent remark: could a boy make a living playing this instrument [a violin] in our competitive civilization today?' Roxy: 'I think I'll run across the street and pick up an eight-cylinder sandwich.'

The audiences roared with delight at these inventions. It was as though Odets was trying to turn dialogue into jazz.

And his devotees went to his plays especially to pick up his latest deliciously improbable remarks and repeat them to their friends. Had any Bronxite – or anyone else in the century – really exclaimed, 'God's teeth, no!' 'What exhaust-pipe did he crawl out of?' 'I feel like I'm shot from a cannon.'

Inevitably, in a theatre bounded by realism this had to be mistakenly labelled as simply a kind of accurate reportage, news from the netherworld. But of course it was an invented diction with slashes of imagery, of a kind never heard before on-stage or off for that matter. Odets' fervent ambition was to burst the bounds of Broadway while remaining inside its embrace, and if as time went on his lines began to seem self-consciously laboured, no longer springing from characters but manifestly from the author and his will-to-poeticize, he at a minimum had made language the identifying mark of a playwright in America, and that was something that hadn't happened before.

Admittedly, I could not look at his style with objectivity but for its potential usefulness in breaking through the constricted realism of our theatre then. Odets was tremendously exciting to young writers. I was troubled by a tendency in his plays to over-theatricalized excess, however – lines sometimes brought laughter where there should have been outrage, or pity or some deeper emotion than amusement, and at times the plots verged on the schematic. There was often a certain over-rhapsodizing at the climaxes when there should have been a reaching back to ancillary material that was not there. Odets wrote terrific scenes, blazing speeches and confrontations which showed what theatre could be but, with the exception perhaps of *Rocket to the Moon*, not a finished play lifting inexorably to its climactic revelation.

I came out of the thirties unsure whether there could be a viable counter-form to the realism around me. All I

knew for sure was that a good play must move forward in
its depths as rapidly as on its surfaces; word-poetry wasn't
enough if there was a fractured poetry in the structure, the
gradually revealed illuminating idea behind the whole
thing. A real play was the discovery of the unity of its
contradictions, the essential poetry was the synthesis of
even the least of its parts to form a symbolic meaning. Of
course the problem had much to do with language but
more primary was how to penetrate my own feelings about
myself and the time in which I lived. Ideally, a good play
must show as sound an emotional proof of its thesis as a
case at law does factually, and you couldn't really do that
with words alone, lovely as they might be.

Odets' contribution, ironically, was not his realistic
portrayal of social reality – his alleged aim – but his
willingness to be artificial; he brought back artificiality, if
you will, just as ten years later Tennessee Williams did
with his birdsong from the magnolias. But Williams had
an advantage – his language could be far more faithful to
its sources in reality. Southern people did love to talk, and
in these accents much like –

AMANDA. . . . But Laura is, thank heavens, not only
   pretty but also very domestic. I'm not at all. I never
   was a bit. I never could make a thing but angel-food
   cake. Well, in the South we had so many servants.
   Gone, gone, gone. All vestige of gracious living! Gone
   completely! I wasn't prepared for what the future
   brought me. All my gentlemen callers were sons of
   planters and so of course I assumed that I would be
   married to one and raise my family on a large piece of
   land with plenty of servants. But man proposes – and
   woman accepts the proposal! – To vary that old, old
   saying a little bit – I married no planter! I married a
   man who worked for the telephone company! – That
   gallantly smiling gentleman over there! (*Points to*

husband's picture.) A telephone man who – fell in love
with long distance! Now he travels and I don't even
know where! . . .

This too was called realism, and it probably was in the
sense that there were people who talked like this. But then
how did it differ from the conventional realistic play?
Clearly, it was that the very action of his plays, certainly
the best of them, was working toward the building of
symbolic meaning that would embrace both the
psychological development of his characters and his
personal spectre of a menacing America struggling with its
own sexuality and the anomie born of its dire materialism.
In a word, Williams' style arose from his pain and anxiety
at being overwhelmed and defeated by a gross violence
that underlay the American – one might say the whole
Western – ethos.

Their obsession with words notwithstanding, it was
their need to communicate their resistance to something
death-dealing in the culture that finally pressed Odets and
Williams to address the big public and made them
playwrights rather than sequestered poets. Stylistic
invention without an implicit commitment of some kind to
a more humane vision of life is a boat without rudder or
cargo or destination, or worse, the occupation of the
dilettante. Odets, when he began, thought his egalitarian
Marxism would heal America and create its new
community, but it devolved into a rote religion before the
thirties had even passed. Williams unfurled the banner of
a forlorn but resisting heroism to the violence against the
oddball, the poet, the sexual dissident. But it may as well
be admitted that in their different ways both men in the
end unwittingly collaborated with the monster they saw as
trying to destroy them.

Their plays for both these men were shields raised
against the many-arrowed darkness, but in the end there

was little from outside to give them the spiritual support to complete their creative lives. Odets' creativity ended with his rejection by Broadway and his move to Hollywood; Williams, likewise rejected, kept nevertheless to his trade, experimenting with forms and new methods that drew no echo from reviewers unable or unwilling to notice that the theatre culture had boxed in a writer of greatness, who was struggling to find an audience in the passing crowd of another generation than his own. At his strongest he had spoken for and to the centre of society and in a style it could relate to, an enhanced, visionary realism. In the end a writer has no one to blame for his failings, not even himself, but the brutally dismissive glee of critics toward Williams' last plays simply laid more sticks on his burden. Toward the end he was still outside scratching on the glass, as he had once put it, and it was the shadowed edges of life that drew him, the borderland where how things are said is everything, and everything has been said before.

The advent of the Absurd and of Beckett and his followers both obscured and illuminated the traditional elements of the discussion of theatre style. For O'Neill, as an example, a good style was basically a question of the apt use of metaphor and argot. 'God, if I could write like that!' he wrote to O'Casey, who, incidentally, would no doubt have labelled himself a realistic writer in the sense that he was giving his audiences the substance of their life-conflicts. But like Williams, O'Casey came from a culture which loved talk and sucked on language like a sweet candy.

> MRS GOGAN. Oh, you've got a cold on you, Fluther.
> FLUTHER. Oh, it's only a little one.
> MRS GOGAN. You'd want to be careful, all th' same. I knew a woman, a big lump of a woman, red-faced and round-bodied, a little awkward on her feet; you'd think, to look at her, she could put out her two arms

an' lift a two-storied house on th' top of her head; got
a ticklin' in her throat, an' a little cough, an' th' next
mornin' she had a little catchin' in her chest, an' they
had just time to wet her lips with a little rum, an' off
she went.

Even in the most mundane of conversational exchanges
O'Casey sought and as often as not found the lift of
poetry. Indeed, that was the whole point – that the
significantly poetic sprang from the raw and real
experience of ordinary people. J.M. Synge, O'Casey's
forerunner at the turn of the century, had struck a similar
chord; Synge was in a supremely conscious revolt against
the banality of most theatre language. As John Gassner
noted, in Ireland, according to Synge, the popular
imagination was still 'fiery and magnificent, and tender; so
that those of us who wish to write start with a chance that
is not given to writers in places where the springtime of
local life has been forgotten, and the harvest is a memory
only, and the straw has been turned into bricks.'

Synge rejected the then-dominant Ibsen and Zola for
their realism with 'joyless and pallid words', and instead,
as in *Riders to the Sea* when the women are lamenting
the deaths of so many of their men working the angry
sea –

MAURYA. In the big world the old people do be leaving
things after them for their sons and children, but in
this place it is the young men do be leaving things
behind for them that do be old.

As far as style is concerned, the Beckett difference, as it
might be called, was to introduce humble people, bums,
in fact, or social sufferers, with the plainest of language,
but arranged so as to announce and develop pure theme.
His could be called a presentational thematic play,
announcing what it was about and never straying very

far from its theme. Beckett had parted with inferential playwriting, where speeches inferred the author's thematic intentions while cleaving to an apparently autonomous story, which builds to a revelatory climax bringing story and theme together. In Beckett the story *was* the theme, inseparably so. Moreover, as will be shown in a moment, he interpreted it himself in his dialogue.

If, instead of the pre-war poetic drama's requirement of an elevated tone or diction, the most common speech was now prized, it was not the speech of realistic plays. It was a speech skewed almost out of recognition by a surreal commitment to what at first had seemed to me the impotence of human hopes, and hence the futility of action itself. All but the flimsiest connectiveness between speeches was eliminated, creating an atmosphere of sinister danger (in Pinter) or (in Beckett) immanence. It was quite as though the emphatic absence of purpose in the characters had created a loss of syntax. I take it that in later years Beckett took pains to clarify this impression of human futility, emphasizing the struggle *against* inertia as his theme. In any case, however ridiculous so much of his dialogue exchanges are, the tenderness of feeling in his work is emphatically not that of the cynic or the mere ironist.

The dominating theme of *Godot* being stasis and the struggle to overcome humanity's endlessly repetitious paralysis before the need to act and change, we hear it plainly and stripped clean of plot or even incident.

ESTRAGON. Then adieu.

POZZO. Adieu.

VLADIMIR. Adieu.

POZZO. Adieu.

 Silence. No one moves.

VLADIMIR. Adieu.

POZZO. Adieu.

ESTRAGON. Adieu.

Silence.

POZZO. And thank you.

VLADIMIR. Thank *you*.

POZZO. Not at all.

ESTRAGON. Yes yes.

POZZO. No no.

VLADIMIR. Yes yes.

ESTRAGON. No no.

Silence.

POZZO. I don't seem to be able . . . (*Long hesitation.*) . . . to depart.

ESTRAGON. Such is life.

This is a vaudeville at the edge of the cliff, but vaudeville anyway, so I may be forgiven for being reminded of Jimmy Durante's ditty – 'Didja ever get the feelin' that you wanted to go? But you wanted to stay? But you wanted to go?'

It is a language shorn of metaphor, simile, everything but its instructions, so to speak, for the listener to hear the theme like a nail drawn across a pane of glass.

So the struggle with what might be called reportorial realism, written 'the way people talk', is at least as old as the century. As for myself, my own tendency has been to shift styles according to the nature of my subject. *All My Sons, The Crucible, A View from the Bridge, Death of a Salesman, The Price, The American Clock*, my earliest work like *The Golden Years*, about the destruction of Mexico by the Spaniards, and the more recent plays like *The Creation of the World, Some Kind of Love Story* and *The Last Yankee*, differ very much in their language. This, in order to find speech that springs naturally out of the characters and their backgrounds rather than imposing a general style. If my approach to playwriting is partly literary I hope it is well-hidden. Leroy Hamilton is a native New England carpenter and speaks like one, and not like other

New York working men and women in *A Memory of Two Mondays*, or Eddie Carbone who comes out of a quite different culture.

So the embrace of something called realism is obviously very wide; it can span the distance between a Turgenev and a Becque, between Wedekind and your latest Broadway hit. The main thing I sought in *The Last Yankee* was first to make real my sense of the life of such people, the kind of man swinging the hammer through a lifetime, the kind of woman waiting forever for her ship to come in. And secondly, my view of their present confusion and, if you will, decay and possible recovery. They are bedrock, aspiring not to greatness but to other gratifications – a successful parenthood, decent children and a decent house and a decent car and an occasional nice evening with family or friends, and above all, of course, some financial security. Needless to say, they are people who can be inspired to great and noble sacrifice, but also to bitter hatreds. As the world goes I suppose they are its luckiest people, but some of them – a great many, in fact, have gotten sick with what would once have been called a sickness of the soul.

And that is the subject of the play, its 'matter'. For depression is far from being merely a question of an individual's illness although it appears as that, of course; it is at the same time, most especially in Patricia Hamilton's case, the grip on her of a success mythology which is both naive and brutal, and which to her misfortune, she has made her own. And opposing it, quite simply, is her husband Leroy's incredibly enduring love for her, for nature and the world.

A conventionally realistic play would no doubt have attempted to create a 'just-like-life' effect, with the sickness gradually rising out of the normal routines of the family's life, and calling up our empathy by virtue of our instant identification with familiar reality. But while

Patricia Hamilton, the carpenter's wife, is seen as an
individual sufferer the context of her illness is equally
important because, for one thing, she knows, as do many
such patients, that more Americans (and West Europeans)
are in hospitals for depression than any other ailment. In
life, with such people, a high degree of objectification or
distancing exists, and the style of the play had to reflect
the fact that they commonly know a great deal about the
social setting of the illness even as they are unable to tear
themselves free of it. And this affects the play's style.

It opens by directly, even crudely grasping the core of
its central preoccupation – the moral and social myths
feeding the disease; and we have a discussion of the
hospital's enormous parking lot, a conversation bordering
on the absurd. I would call this realism, but it is far from
the tape-recorded kind. Frick, like Leroy Hamilton, has
arrived for a visit with his wife, and after a moment's
silence while the two strangers grope for a conversational
opening . . .

FRICK. Tremendous parking space down there. They
    need that for?
LEROY. Well a lot of people visit on weekends. Fills up
    pretty much.
FRICK. Really? That whole area?
LEROY. Pretty much.
FRICK. Doubt that.

The play is made of such direct blows aimed at the
thematic centre; there is a vast parking space because
crowds of stricken citizens converge on this place to visit
mothers, fathers, brothers and sisters. So that the two
patients we may be about to meet are not at all unique.
This is in accord with the vision of the play, which is
intended to be both close-up and wide, psychological and
social, subjective and objective, and manifestly so. To be
sure there is a realistic tone to this exchange, people do

indeed seem to talk this way, but an inch below is the
thematic selectivity which drives the whole tale. Perhaps it
needs to be said that this split vision has informed all the
plays I have written. I have tried to make things seen in
their social context and simultaneously felt as intimate
testimony, and that requires a style, but one that draws as
little attention to itself as possible, for I would wish a play
to be absorbed rather than merely observed.

I have called this play a comedy, a comedy about a
tragedy and I am frankly not sure why. Possibly it is due
to the absurdity of people constantly comparing
themselves to others – something we all do to one degree
or another, but in Patricia's case to the point of illness.

PATRICIA. There was something else you said. About
　standing on line.
LEROY. On line?
PATRICIA. That you'll always be at the head of the line
　because . . . (*Breaks off.*)
LEROY. I'm the only one on it . . . We're really all on a
　one-person line, Pat. I learned that in these years.

The play's language, then, has a surface of everyday realism,
but its action is overtly stylized rather than 'natural'.

Finally, a conventionally realistic work about mental
illness would be bound to drive to a reverberating climax.
But repression is the cultural inheritance of these New
Englanders and such theatricality would be a betrayal of
their style of living and dying. Indeed, short of suicide, the
illness properly speaking never ends in the sense of tying
all the loose strings, nor should the play, which simply
sets the boundaries of the possible. For the theme is hope
rather than completion or achievement, and hope is
tentative always. A play about them should have a certain
amplitude of sound, nothing greater or less, reflecting
their tight yet often deeply felt culture. And in a play
about them they should recognize themselves, and even

possibly what drives them mad. That would be a satisfactory realism as I see it – just like the longshoremen who saw themselves in *A View from the Bridge* or the cops in *The Price* or the salespeople in *Death of a Salesman*.

I suppose the form itself of *The Last Yankee* is as astringently direct and uncluttered as it is because these people are supremely the prey of the culture, if only because it is never far from the centre of their minds – the latest film or TV show, the economy's ups and downs, and above all the endless advertising-encouraged self-comparisons with others who are more or less successful than they. This ritualistic preoccupation is at the play's dramatic core and, I felt, ought not be unclear or misted over, for it is from its grip they must be freed if they are ever to be free at all. Hence, the repeated references to ambition, to success and failure, to wealth and poverty, to economic survival, to the kind of car one drives and the suit one wears. In a word, the play could not be amorphously 'realistic' if it was to reflect the obsessiveness of the characters in life. So if *The Last Yankee* is realism it is of this kind resulting from an intense selectivity which in turn is derived from the way these people live and feel.

But obviously, to make such a strictly thematic play demands intense condensation and the syncopating of idea and feeling and language. More than one actor in my plays has told me that it is surprisingly difficult to memorize their dialogue. It sounds like real, almost reported talk when in fact it is intensely composed, compressed, 'angled' into an inevitability that seems natural but isn't. But it is always necessary to employ the artificial in order to arrive at the real. So that for me at any rate, the question I bring to a play is not whether its form and style are new or old, experimental or traditional, but first, whether it brings news, something truly felt by its author, something thought through to its conclusion and its significance; and secondly, whether the economy of its form is beautiful, economic, or wasteful; whether it is aberrant for aberrancy's sake, full of surprises that discover little, and so on.

Something called Realism can land us further from common reality than the most fantastic caprice. But in the end, if stylization in theatre needs justification, and it does of course, it is not its novelty but its enhancement of discovery of how life works in our time. How a thing is said is therefore only as important as what it is saying. The proof is the deep pile of experimental plays of two, three, five, ten years ago, which can only be appreciated any more by the scholar-specialist. It is a pile, incidentally, no smaller than the one for so many realistic plays of the same era. So finding the truth is no easier now when we are totally free to use any stylistic means at hand than it was a century or half a century ago when a play had to be 'real' even to be read, and had to make sense to sensible people. Ultimately every assault on the human mystery falls back to the ground, changing little, but the flight of the arrow continues claiming our attention over a longer time when its direction is toward the castle rather than the wayward air.

Arthur Miller
1994

The Last Yankee

The Last Yankee received its British première at the Young Vic Theatre, London on 26 January 1993, with the following cast:

FRICK	David Healy
LEROY	Peter Davison
PATRICIA	Zoë Wanamaker
KAREN	Helen Burns
PATIENT	Bethany Hanson

Directed by David Thacker
Set design Shelagh Keegan
Costume design Helen Skillicorn
Lighting design Jim Simmons
Movement Lesley Hutchison

The play transferred to the Duke of York's, London on 20 April 1993 with Margot Leicester as Patricia.

Scene One

The visiting room of a state mental hospital. LEROY HAMILTON *is seated on one of the half-dozen chairs idly leafing through an old magazine. He is forty-eight, trim, dressed in subdued Ivy League jacket and slacks and shined brogans. A banjo case rests against his chair.*

MR FRICK *enters. He is sixty, solid, in a business suit. He carries a small valise. He looks about, glances at* LEROY, *just barely nods, and sits ten feet away. He looks at his watch, then impatiently at the room.* LEROY *goes on leafing through the magazine.*

FRICK (*pointing right*). Supposed to notify somebody in there?

LEROY (*indicating left*). Did you give your name to the attendant?

FRICK. Yes. Seem to be paying much attention, though.

LEROY. They know you're here, then. He calls through to the ward.

Returns to his magazine.

FRICK (*slight pause*). Tremendous parking space down there. They need that for?

LEROY. Well a lot of people visit on weekends. Fills up pretty much.

FRICK. Really? That whole area?

LEROY. Pretty much.

FRICK. Doubt that.

He goes to the window and looks out. Pause.

Beautifully landscaped, got to say that for it.

LEROY. Yes, it's a very nice place.

FRICK. See them walking around out there it's hard to tell. Stopped one to ask directions and only realized when he stuck out his finger and pointed at my nose.

LEROY. Heh-heh.

FRICK. Quite a shock. Sitting there reading some thick book and crazy as a coot. You'd never know.

He sits in another chair. LEROY *returns to the magazine. He studies* LEROY.

Is it your wife?

LEROY. Yes.

FRICK. I've got mine in there too.

LEROY. Uh, huh.

He stares ahead, politely refraining from the magazine.

FRICK. My name's Frick.

LEROY. Hi. I'm Hamilton.

FRICK. Gladameetu.

Slight pause.

How do you find it here?

LEROY. I guess they do a good job.

FRICK. Surprisingly well-kept for a state institution.

LEROY. Oh, ya.

FRICK. Awful lot of colored, though, ain't there?

LEROY. Quite a few, ya.

FRICK. Yours been in long?

LEROY. Going on seven weeks now.

FRICK. They give you any idea when she can get out?

LEROY. Oh, I could take her out now, but I won't for a couple weeks.

FRICK. Why's that?

LEROY. Well this is her third time.

FRICK. Don't say.

LEROY. I'd like them to be a little more sure before I take her out again. . . . Although you can never *be* sure.

FRICK. That fairly common? – that they have to come back?

LEROY. About a third they say. This your first time, I guess.

FRICK. I just brought her in last Tuesday. I certainly hope she doesn't have to stay long. They ever say what's wrong with her?

LEROY. She's a depressive.

FRICK. Really. That's what they say about mine. Just gets . . . sort of sad?

LEROY. It's more like . . . frightened.

FRICK. Sounds just like mine. Got so she wouldn't even leave the house.

LEROY. That's right.

FRICK. Oh, yours too?

LEROY. Ya, she wouldn't go out. Not if she could help it, anyway.

FRICK. She ever hear sounds?

LEROY. She used to. Like a loud humming.

FRICK. Same thing! Ts. What do you know! – How old is she?

LEROY. She's forty-four.

FRICK. Is that all! I had an idea it had something to do with getting old . . .

LEROY. I don't think so. My wife is still – I wouldn't say a raving beauty, but she's still . . . a pretty winsome woman. They're usually sick a long time before you realize it, you know. I just never realized it.

FRICK. Mine never showed any signs at all. Just a nice, quiet kind of a woman. Always slept well . . .

LEROY. Well mine sleeps well too.

FRICK. Really?

LEROY. Lots of them love to sleep. I found that out. She'd take naps every afternoon. Longer and longer.

FRICK. Mine too. But then about six, eight months ago she got nervous about keeping the doors locked. And then the windows. I had to air condition the whole house. I finally had to do the shopping, she just wouldn't go out.

LEROY. Oh, I've done the shopping for twenty years.

FRICK. You don't say!

LEROY. Well, you just never think of it as a sickness. I like to ski, for instance, or ice-skating . . . she'd never come along. Or swimming in the summer. I always took the kids alone . . .

FRICK. Oh you have children.

LEROY. Yes. Seven.

FRICK. Seven! – I've been wondering if it was because she never had any.

LEROY. No, that's not it. – You don't have *any?*

FRICK. No. We kept putting it off, and then it got too late, and first thing you know . . . it's just too late.

LEROY. For a while there I thought maybe she had too *many* children . . .

FRICK. Well I don't have any, so . . .

LEROY. Yeah, I guess that's not it either.

Slight pause.

FRICK. I just can't figure it out. There's no bills; we're very well fixed; she's got a beautiful home . . . There's really not a trouble in the world. Although, God knows, maybe that's the trouble . . .

LEROY. Oh no, I got plenty of bills and it didn't help mine. I don't think it's how many bills you have.

FRICK. What do you think it is, then?

LEROY. Don't ask me, I don't know.

FRICK. When she started locking up everything I thought maybe it's these Negroes, you know? There's an awful lot of fear around; all this crime.

LEROY. I don't think so. My wife was afraid before there were any Negroes. I mean, around.

FRICK. Well, one thing came out of it – I finally learned how to make coffee. And mine's better than hers was. It's an awful sensation, though – coming home and there's nobody there.

LEROY. How'd you like to come home and there's seven of them there?

FRICK. I guess I'm lucky at that.

LEROY. Well, I am too. They're wonderful kids.

FRICK. They still very young?

LEROY. Five to nineteen. But they all pitch in. Everything's clean, house runs like a ship.

FRICK. You're lucky to have good children these days. – I guess we're both lucky.

LEROY. That's the only way to look at it. Start feeling sorry for yourself, that's when you're in trouble.

FRICK. Awfully hard to avoid sometimes.

LEROY. You can't give into it though. Like today – I was so disgusted I just laid down and . . . I was ready to throw in the chips. But then I got up and washed my face, put on the clothes, and here I am. After all, she can't help it either, who are you going to blame?

FRICK. It's a mystery – a woman with everything she could possibly want. I don't care what happens to the country, there's nothing could ever hurt her any more. Suddenly, out of nowhere, she's terrified! . . . She lost all her optimism. Yours do that? Lose her optimism?

LEROY. Mine was never very optimistic. She's Swedish.

FRICK. Oh. Mine certainly was. Whatever deal I was in, couldn't wait till I got home to talk about it. Real estate, stock market, always interested. All of a sudden, no interest whatsoever. Might as well be talking to that wall over there. – Your wife have brothers and sisters?

LEROY. Quite a few, ya.

FRICK. Really. I even thought maybe it's that she was an only child, and if she had brothers and sisters to talk to . . .

LEROY. Oh no – at least I don't think so. It could be even worse.

FRICK. They don't help, huh?

LEROY. They *think* they're helping. Come around saying it's a disgrace for their sister to be in a public institution. That's the kind of help. So I said, 'Well, I'm the public!'

FRICK. Sure! – It's a perfectly nice place.

LEROY. They want her in the Rogers Pavilion.

FRICK. Rogers! – That's a couple of hundred dollars a day minimum . . .

LEROY. Well if I had that kind of money I wouldn't mind, but . . .

FRICK. No-no, don't you do it. I could afford it, but what are we paying taxes for?

LEROY. So they can go around saying their sister's in the Rogers Pavilion, that's all.

FRICK. Out of the question. That's fifty thousand dollars a year. Plus tips. I'm sure you have to tip them there.

LEROY. Besides, it's eighty miles there and back, I could never get to see her . . .

FRICK. If they're so sensitive you ought to tell *them* to play for it. That'd shut them up, I bet.

LEROY. Well no – they've offered to pay part. Most of it, in fact.

FRICK. Whyn't you do it, then?

LEROY (*holding a secret*). I didn't think it's a good place for her.

FRICK. Why? – if they'd pay for it? It's one of the top places in the country. Some very rich people go there.

LEROY. I know.

FRICK. And the top doctors, you know. And they order whatever they want to eat. I went up there to look it over; no question about it, it's absolutely first class, much better than this place. You should take them up on it.

LEROY. I'd rather have her here.

FRICK. Well I admire your attitude. You don't see that kind of pride any more.

LEROY. It's not pride, exactly.

FRICK. Never mind, it's a great thing, keep it up. Everybody's got the gimmes, it's destroying the country. Had a man in a few weeks ago to put in a new shower-head. Nothing to it. Screw off the old one and screw on the new one. Twenty-seven dollars an hour!

LEROY. Yeah, well.

Gets up, unable to remain.

Everybody's got to live, I guess.

FRICK. I take my hat off to you – that kind of independence. Don't happen to be with Colonial Trust, do you?

LEROY. No.

FRICK. There was something familiar about you. What line are you in?

LEROY (*he is at the window now, staring out. Slight pause*). Carpenter.

FRICK (*taken aback*). Don't say. . . . Contractor?

LEROY. No. Just carpenter. – I take on one or two fellas when I have to, but I work alone most of the time.

FRICK. I'd never have guessed it.

LEROY. Well that's what I do.

Looks at his watch wanting escape.

FRICK. I mean your whole . . . your way of dressing and everything.

LEROY. Why? Just ordinary clothes.

FRICK. No, you look like a college man.

LEROY. Most of them have long hair, don't they?

FRICK. The way college men used to look. I've spent thirty years around carpenters, that's why it surprised me. You know Frick Supply, don't you?

LEROY. Oh ya. I've bought quite a lot of wood from Frick.

FRICK. I sold out about five years ago . . .

LEROY. I know. I used to see you around there.

FRICK. You did? Why didn't you mention it?

LEROY (*shrugs*). Just didn't.

FRICK. You say Anthony?

LEROY. No, Hamilton. Leroy.

FRICK (*points at him*). Hey now! Of course! There was a big article about you in the *Herald* a couple of years ago. Descended from Alexander Hamilton.

LEROY. That's right.

FRICK. Sure! No wonder! (*Holding out his palm as to a photo.*) Now that I visualize you in overalls, I think I recognize you. In fact, you were out in the yard loading plywood the morning that article came out. My bookkeeper pointed you out through the window. It's those clothes – if I'd seen you in overalls I'd've recognized you right off. Well, what do you know? (*The air of condescension plus wonder.*) Amazing thing what clothes'll do, isn't it. – Keeping busy?

LEROY. I get work.

FRICK. What are you fellas charging now?

LEROY. I get twenty-seven an hour.

FRICK. Good for you.

LEROY. I hate asking that much but even so I just about make it.

FRICK. Shouldn't feel that way; if they'll pay it grab it.

LEROY. Well ya, but it's still a lot of money. – My head's still back there thirty years ago.

FRICK. What are you working on now?

LEROY. I'm renovating a colonial near Waverly. I just finished over in Belleville. The Presbyterian Church.

FRICK. Did you do *that*?

LEROY. Yeah, just finished Wednesday.

FRICK. That's a beautiful job. You're a good man. Where'd they get that altar?

LEROY. I built that.

FRICK. That altar?

LEROY. Uh huh.

FRICK. Hell, that's first-class! Huh! You must be doing all right.

LEROY. Just keeping ahead of it.

FRICK (*slight pause*). How'd it happen?

LEROY. What's that?

FRICK. Well, coming out of an old family like that – how do you come to being a carpenter?

LEROY. Just . . . liked it.

FRICK. Father a carpenter?

LEROY. No.

FRICK. What was your father?

LEROY. Lawyer.

FRICK. Why didn't you?

LEROY. Just too dumb, I guess.

FRICK. Couldn't buckle down to the books, huh?

LEROY. I guess not.

FRICK. Your father should've taken you in hand.

LEROY (*sits with magazine, opening it*). He didn't like the law either.

FRICK. Even so. – Many of the family still around?

LEROY. Well, my mother, and two brothers.

FRICK. No, I mean of the Hamiltons.

LEROY. Well they're Hamiltons.

FRICK. I know, but I mean – some of them must be pretty important people.

LEROY. I wouldn't know. I never kept track of them.

FRICK. You should. Probably some of them must be pretty big. – Never even looked them up?

LEROY. Nope.

FRICK (*slight pause*). You realize the importance of Alexander Hamilton, don't you?

LEROY. I know about him, more or less.

FRICK. More or less! He was one of the most important Founding Fathers.

LEROY. I guess so, ya.

FRICK. You read about him, didn't you?

LEROY. Well sure . . . I read about him.

FRICK. Well didn't your father talk about him?

LEROY. Some. But he didn't care for him much.

FRICK. Didn't care for *Alexander Hamilton*?

LEROY. It was something to do with his philosophy. But I never kept up with the whole thing.

FRICK (*laughing, shaking his head*). Boy, you're quite a character, aren't you.

LEROY *is silent, reddening.* FRICK *continues chuckling at him for a moment.*

LEROY. I hope to God your wife is cured, Mr Frick, I hope she never has to come back here again.

FRICK (*sensing the hostility*). What have I said?

LEROY. This is the third time in two years for mine, and I don't mean to be argumentative but it's got me right at the end of my rope. For all I know I'm in line for this funny farm myself by now, but I have to tell you that this could be what's driving so many people crazy.

FRICK. What is!

LEROY. This.

FRICK. This what?

LEROY. This whole kind of conversation.

FRICK. Why? What's wrong with it?

LEROY. Well never mind.

FRICK. I don't know what you're talking about.

LEROY. Well what's it going to be, equality or what kind of country? – I mean am I supposed to be ashamed I'm a carpenter?

FRICK. Who said you. . . ?

LEROY. Then why do you talk like this to a man? One minute my altar is terrific and the next minute I'm some kind of shit bucket.

FRICK. Hey now, wait a minute . . .

LEROY. I don't mean anything against you personally, I know you're a successful man and more power to you, but this whole type of conversation about my clothes – should I be ashamed I'm a carpenter? I mean everybody's talking 'labor, labor,' how much labor's getting; well if it's so great to be labor how come nobody wants to be it? I mean you ever hear a parent going around saying (*Mimes thumb pridefully tucked into suspenders.*) 'My son is a carpenter?' Do you? Do you ever hear people brag about a bricklayer? I don't know what you are but I'm only a dumb swamp Yankee, but . . . (*Suddenly breaks off with a shameful laugh.*) Excuse me. I'm really sorry. But you come back here two-three more times and you're liable to start talking the way you were never brought up to. (*Opens magazine.*)

FRICK. I don't understand what you're so hot about.

LEROY (*looks up from the magazine. Seems to start to explain, then sighs*). Nothing.

He returns to his magazine. FRICK *shakes his head with a certain condescension, then goes back to the window and looks out.*

FRICK. It's one hell of a parking lot, you have to say that for it.

They sit down for a long moment in silence, each in his own thoughts.

Blackout

Scene Two

Most of the stage is occupied by Patricia's bedroom. In one of the beds a fully clothed PATIENT *lies motionless with one arm over her eyes. She will not move throughout the scene.*

Outside this bedroom is a corner of the Recreation Room, bare but for a few scattered chairs.

Presently . . . from just offstage the sound of a ping-pong game. The ball comes bouncing into the Recreation Room area and PATRICIA HAMILTON *enters chasing it. She captures it and with a sigh of boredom goes offstage with it. The* PATIENT *is oblivious.*

We hear two or three pings and the ball comes onstage again with PATRICIA HAMILTON *after it. She starts to return to the game offstage but halts, looks at the ball in her hand, and to someone offstage . . .*

PATRICIA. Why are we doing this? Come let's talk, I hate these games.

MRS KAREN FRICK *enters. She is in her sixties, very thin, eyeglasses, wispy hair.*

I said I'm quitting.

KAREN *stares at the paddle.*

Well, never mind. (*Studies her watch.*) You're very good.

KAREN. My sister-in-law taught me. She used to be a stewardess on the Queen Mary. She could even play when the ship was rocking. But she never married.

PATRICIA. Here, put it down, dear.

KAREN *passively gives up the paddle, then stands there looking uncomfortable.*

PATRICIA. I'm going to lie down in my room; come in if you like.

KAREN. Hardly anyone ever seems to come out here.

PATRICIA. They don't like exercise, they're too depressed.

They enter the bedroom. PATRICIA *lies down. The* PATIENT *in the other bed does not stir and no attention is paid to her.*

PATRICIA. Don't feel obliged to say anything if you . . .

KAREN. I get sick to my stomach just looking at a boat. Does your husband hunt?

PATRICIA. Sit down. Relax yourself. You don't have to talk. Although I think you're doing a little better than yesterday.

KAREN. Oh, I like talking with you. (*Explaining herself timorously; indicating offstage – and very privately . . .*) I should go out – he doesn't like being kept waiting, don't y'know.

PATRICIA. Why are you so afraid? He might start treasuring you more if you make him wait a little. Come, sit.

KAREN *adventurously sits at the foot of the bed, glancing about nervously.*

Men are only big children, you know – give them a chocolate soda every day and pretty soon it doesn't mean a thing to them. (*Looks at her watch again.*) Only reason I'm nervous is that I can't decide whether to go home today. – But you mustn't mention it, will you?

KAREN. Mention . . ?

PATRICIA. About my pills. I haven't told anybody yet.

KAREN *looks a bit blank.*

Well never mind.

KAREN. Oh! You mean not taking them.

PATRICIA. But you mustn't mention it, will you. The doctor would be very upset.

KAREN. And how long has it been?

PATRICIA. Twenty-one days today. It's the longest I've been clean in maybe fifteen years. I can hardly believe it.

KAREN. Are you Baptist?

PATRICIA. Baptist? No, we're more Methodist. But the church I'd really love hasn't been invented yet.

KAREN (*charmed, slavishly interested*). How would it be?

PATRICIA (*begins to describe it, breaks off*). I can't describe it. (*A sigh of lostness.*) I was raised Lutheran, of course. – But I often go to the Marble Baptist Church on Route 91? I've gotten to like that minister. – You hear what I'm saying, don't you?

KAREN *looks at her nervously trying to remember.*

I must say it's kind of relaxing talking to you, Karen, knowing that you probably won't remember too much. But you'll come out of it all right, you're just a little scared, aren't you. – But who isn't?

Slight pause.

Doctor Rockwell is not going to believe I'm doing better without medication but I really think something's clicked inside me. (*A deep breath.*) I even seem to be breathing easier. And I'm not feeling that sort of fuzziness in my head. – It's like some big bird has been hovering over me for fifteen years, and suddenly it's flown away.

KAREN. I can't stand dead animals, can you?

PATRICIA. Well just insist that he has to stop hunting! You don't have to stand for that, you're a *person*.

KAREN. Well, you know, men like to . . .

PATRICIA. Not all – I've known some lovely men. Not many, but a few. This minister I mentioned? He came one day this summer and sat with me on our porch . . . and we had ice cream and talked for over an hour. You know, when he left his previous church they gave him a Pontiac Grand Am. He made me realize something; he said that I seem to be in like a constant state of prayer. And it's true; every once in a while it stops me short, realizing it. It's like inside me I'm almost continually talking to the Lord. (*Deeply excited, but suppressing it.*) I tell you truthfully, if I can really come out of this I'm going to . . . I don't know what . . . fall in love with God. I think I have already.

KAREN. You're really beautiful.

PATRICIA. Oh no, dear, I'm a torn-off rag of my old self. The pills put ten years on my face. If he was a Jew or Italian or even Irish he'd be suing these doctors, but Yankees never sue, you know. Although I have to say the only thing he's been right about is medication.

KAREN. Your husband against pills?

PATRICIA. Fanatical. But of course he can stick his head out the window and go high as a kite on a breath of fresh air. (*Looks at her watch.*)

KAREN. I really think you're extremely attractive.

PATRICIA. No-no dear, although I did win the county beauty pageant when I was nineteen. But if you're talking beauty you should have seen my mother. She only died two years ago, age eighty-nine but I still haven't gotten over it. On the beach, right into her seventies, people would still be staring at her – she had an unbelievable bust right up to the end.

KAREN. I cut this finger once in a broken Coke machine. But we never sued.

PATRICIA. Did your conversation always jump around? Because it could be your pills, believe me; the soul belongs to God, we're not supposed to be stuffing Prozac into his mouth.

KAREN. I have a cousin who went right through the windshield and she didn't get a cent.

Slight pause.

And it was five below zero out.

Slight pause.

Her husband's Norwegian.

PATRICIA. Look, dear, I know you're trying but don't feel you have to speak.

KAREN. No, I like speaking to you. Is he Baptist too, your husband?

PATRICIA. I said Methodist. But he's more Episcopal. But he'll go to any church, if it's raining.

Slight pause. A deepening agitation.

I just don't know whether to tell him yet.

KAREN. What?

PATRICIA. That I'm off everything.

KAREN. But he'll like that, won't he?

PATRICIA. Oh yes. But he's going to be doubtful. – Which I am, too, let's face it – I've been on one medication or another for almost twenty years. But I do feel a thousand per cent better. And I really have no idea how it happened. (*Shakes her head.*) Dear God, when I think of him hanging-in there all these years . . . I'm so ashamed. But at the same time he's absolutely refused to make any money, every one of our children has had to work since they could practically write their names. I can't be expected to applaud, exactly. (*Presses her eyes.*) I guess sooner or later you just have to stand up and say, 'I'm normal, I made it.' But it's like standing on top of a stairs and there's no stairs. (*Staring ahead.*)

KAREN. I think I'd better go out to him. Should I tell your husband you're coming out?

PATRICIA. I think I'll wait a minute.

KAREN (*stands*). He seems very nice.

PATRICIA. – I'll tell you the truth, dear – I've put him through hell and I know it . . . (*Tears threaten her.*) I know I have to stop blaming him; it came to me like a visitation two weeks ago, I-must-not-blame-Leroy-anymore. And it's amazing, I lost all desire for medication, I could feel it leaving me like a . . . like a ghost.

Slight pause.

It's just that he's got really well-to-do relatives and he simply will not accept anyone's help. I mean you take the Jews, the Italians, Irish – they've got their Italian-Americans, Irish-Americans, Hispanic-Americans – they stick together and help each other. But you ever hear of Yankee-Americans? Not on your life. Raise his taxes, rob him blind, the Yankee'll just sit there all alone getting sadder and sadder. – But I'm not going to think about it anymore.

KAREN. You have a very beautiful chin.

PATRICIA. Men with half his ability riding around in big expensive cars and now for the second Easter Sunday in a row his rear-end collapsed.

KAREN. I think my license must have expired.

PATRICIA (*a surge of deep anger*). I refuse to ride around in a nine-year-old Chevrolet which was bought second-hand in the first place!

KAREN. They say there are only three keys for all General Motors cars. You suppose that's possible?

PATRICIA (*peremptorily now*). Believe me, dear, whatever they tell you, you have got to cut down the medication. It could be what's making your mind jump around . . .

KAREN. No, it's that you mentioned Chevrolet, which is General Motors, you see.

PATRICIA. Oh. . . . Well, let's just forget about it.

Slight pause.

Although you're probably right – here you're carefully locking your car and some crook is walking around with the same keys in his pocket. But everything's a fake, we all know that.

KAREN (*facing* PATRICIA *again*). I guess that would be depressing.

PATRICIA. No, that's not what depressed me . . .

KAREN. No, I meant him refusing to amount to anything and then spending money on banjo lessons.

PATRICIA. Did I tell you that? – I keep forgetting what I told you because I never know when you're listening. (*Holds out her hand.*) Here we go again. (*Grasps her hand to stop the shaking.*)

KAREN. – You sound like you had a wonderful courtship.

PATRICIA. Oh, Karen, everyone envied us, we were the handsomest pair in town; and I'm not boasting, believe me. (*Breaks off; watches her hand shake and covers it again.*) I just don't want to have to come back here again, you see. I don't think I could bear that. (*Grips her hand, moving about.*) I simply have to think positively. But it's unbelievable – he's seriously talking about donating his saw and chisel collection to the museum! – some of those tools are as old as the United States, they might be worth a fortune! – But I'm going to look ahead, that's all, just as straight ahead as a highway.

Slight pause.

KAREN. I feel so ashamed.

PATRICIA. For Heaven's sake, why? You've got a right to be depressed. There's more people in hospitals because of depression than any other disease.

KAREN. Is that true?

PATRICIA. Of course! Anybody with any sense has got to be depressed in this country. Unless you're really rich, I suppose. Don't let him shame you, dear.

KAREN. No . . . it's that you have so many thoughts.

PATRICIA. Oh. Well, you can have thoughts, too – just remember your soul belongs to God and you mustn't be shoving pills into his mouth.

Slight pause.

KAREN. We're rich, I think.

PATRICIA (*quickly interested*). . . . Really rich?

KAREN. He's got the oil delivery now, and of course he always had the fertilizer and the Chevy dealership, and of course the lumber yard and all. And Izuzu's now.

PATRICIA. What's Izuzus?

KAREN. It's a Japanese car.

PATRICIA. . . . I'll just never catch up.

KAREN. We go to Arkansas in the spring.

PATRICIA. Arkansas?

KAREN. For the catfish. It's where I broke down. But I can't help it, the sight of catfish makes me want to vomit. Not that I was trying to . . . you know . . . do anything. I just read the instructions on the bottle wrong. Do you mind if I ask you something?

PATRICIA. I hope it's nothing personal, is it?

KAREN. Well, I don't know.

PATRICIA. . . . Well go ahead, what is it?

KAREN. Do you shop in the A&P or Stop & Shop?

PATRICIA. . . . I'm wondering if you've got the wrong medication. But I guess you'll never overdose – you vomit at the drop of a hat. It may be your secret blessing.

KAREN. – He wants to get me out of the house more, but it's hard to make up my mind where.

PATRICIA. Well . . . A&P is good. Or Stop & Shop. More or less. Krogers is good for fish sometimes.

KAREN. Which do you like best? I'll go where you go.

PATRICIA. You're very flattering. (*Stands, inner excitement.*) It's amazing – I'm really beginning to feel wonderful, maybe I ought to go home with him today. I mean what does it come down to, really? – it's simply a question of confidence . . .

KAREN. I wish we could raise some vegetables like we did on the farm. Do you?

PATRICIA. Oh, he raises things in our yard. Healthy things like salsify and collards – and kale. You ever eat kale?

KAREN. I can't remember kale.

PATRICIA. You might as well salt your shower curtain and chop it up with a tomato.

KAREN. – So . . . meats are . . . which? – A&P?

PATRICIA. No. Meats are Stop & Shop. I'm really thinking I might go home today. It's just not his fault. I have to remember that . . .

KAREN. But staples?

PATRICIA. What? – Oh. Stop & Shop.

KAREN. Then what's A&P for?

PATRICIA. Vegetables.

KAREN. Oh right. And Krogers?

PATRICIA. Why don't you just forget Krogers.

KAREN (*holds up five fingers, bends one at a time* . . .) Then Stop & Shop . . .

PATRICIA. Maybe it's that you're trying to remember three things. Whyn't you just do A&P and Stop & Shop?

Slight pause.

KAREN. I kind of liked Krogers.

PATRICIA. Then go to Krogers, for heaven's sake!

KAREN. Well, I guess I'll go out to him. (*Moves to go. Halts.*) I hope you aren't really leaving today, are you?

PATRICIA (*higher tension*). I'm deciding.

KAREN. Well . . . here I go, I guess. (*Halts again.*) I meant to tell you, I kind of like the banjo. It's very good with tap-dancing.

PATRICIA. Tap-dancing.

KAREN. There's a tap teacher lives in our road.

PATRICIA. You tap-dance?

KAREN. Well John rented a video of Ginger Rogers and Fred Astaire, and I kind of liked it. I can sing 'Cheek to Cheek'? Would you like to hear it?

PATRICIA. Sure, go ahead – this is certainly a surprise.

KAREN (*sings in a frail voice*). 'Heaven, I'm in heaven, and the cares that clung around me through the week . . .'

PATRICIA. That's beautiful, Karen! Listen, what exactly does Doctor Rockwell say about you?

KAREN. Well, he says it's quite common when a woman is home alone all day.

PATRICIA. What's common?

KAREN. Someone moving around in the next room?

PATRICIA. Oh, I see. – You have any idea who it is?

KAREN. My mother. – My husband might bring my tap shoes and tails . . . but he probably forgot. I have a high hat and shorts too. And a walking stick? But would they allow dancing in here?

PATRICIA. They might. But of course the minute they see you enjoying yourself they'll probably try to knock you out with a pill.

KAREN makes to go, stalls and halts again.

KAREN. Did your mother like you?

PATRICIA. Oh yes. We were all very close. Didn't yours?

KAREN. No. She left the whole farm to her cousin. Tell about your family, can you? Were they really all blond?

PATRICIA. Oh as blond as the tassels on Golden Bantam corn . . . everybody'd turn and look when we went by. My mother was perfection. We all were, I guess. (*With a chuckle.*) You know, we had a flat roof extending from the house over the garage, and mother and my sisters and me – on the first warm spring days we used to sunbathe out there.

KAREN (*covering her mouth*). No! You mean nude?

PATRICIA. Nudity doesn't matter that much in Sweden, and we were all brought up to love the sun. And we'd near die laughing because the minute we dropped our robes – you know how quiet a town Grenville is – you could hear the footsteps going up to the clock tower over the Presbyterian Church, and we pretended not to notice but that little narrow tower was just packed with Presbyterians.

KAREN. Good lord!

PATRICIA. We'd stretch out and pretend not to see a thing.

And then my mother'd sit up suddenly and point up at the steeple and yell, 'Boo!' And they'd all go running down the stairs like mice!

They both enjoy the laugh.

KAREN. I think your husband's very good looking, isn't he?

PATRICIA. He is, but my brothers . . . I mean the way they stood, and walked . . . and their teeth! Charles won the All New England golf tournament, and Buzz came within a tenth of an inch of the gold medal in the pole vault – that was in the Tokyo Olympics.

KAREN. My! Do you still get together much?

PATRICIA. Oh, they're all gone now.

KAREN. Moved away?

PATRICIA. No . . . dead.

KAREN. Oh my. They overstrain?

PATRICIA. Buzz hung himself on his wife's closet door.

KAREN. Oh my!

PATRICIA. Eight days later Charles shot himself on his tractor.

KAREN (*softly*). Oh my. Did they leave a note or anything?

PATRICIA. No. But we all knew what it was.

KAREN. Can you say?

PATRICIA. Disappointment. We were all brought up expecting to be wonderful, and . . . (*Breaks off with a shrug.*) just wasn't.

KAREN. Well . . . here I go.

KAREN *exits.* PATRICIA *stares ahead for a moment in a blankly reminiscent mood. Now she looks at her face in a mirror, smoothing wrinkles away . . .*

LEROY *enters.*

PATRICIA. I was just coming out.

LEROY. 'Cause Mrs Frick . . .

PATRICIA (*cuts him off by drawing his head down and stroking his cheek. And in soft but faintly patronizing tone . . .*). I was just coming out, Leroy. You don't have to repeat everything. Come, sit with me and let's not argue.

LEROY. . . . How's your day been?

She is still moved by her brothers' memory; also, she hasn't received something she hoped for from him. She shrugs and turns her head away.

PATRICIA. I've had worse.

LEROY. Did you wash your hair?

PATRICIA (*pleased he noticed*). How can you tell?

LEROY. Looks livelier. Is that nail polish?

PATRICIA. M-hm.

LEROY. Good. You're looking good, Patty.

PATRICIA. I'm feeling better. Not completely but a lot.

LEROY (*nods approvingly*). Great! Did he change your medication or something?

PATRICIA. No.

LEROY. Something different about you.

PATRICIA (*mysteriously excited*). You think so?

LEROY. Your eyes are clearer. You seem more like you're . . . connecting.

PATRICIA. I am, I think. But I warn you, I'm nervous.

LEROY. That's okay. Your color is more . . . I don't know . . . vigorous.

PATRICIA. Is it? (*She touches her face.*)

LEROY. You look almost like years ago . . .

PATRICIA. Something's happened but I don't want to talk about it yet.

LEROY. Really? Like what?

PATRICIA (*instant resistance*). I just said I . . .

LEROY . . . (*Goes to a window*). – It still looks like rain outside, but we can walk around if you like. They've got a beautiful tulip bed down there; the colors really shine in this gray light. Reds and purple and whites, and a gray. Never saw a tulip be that kind of gray.

PATRICIA. How's Amelia's leg? Are you getting her to change her bandage?

LEROY. Yes. But she'd better stop thinking she can drive a car.

PATRICIA. Well, why don't you tell her?

LEROY (*a little laugh*). That'll be the day, won't it, when she starts listening to her father.

PATRICIA (*a softness despite her language*). She might if you laid down the law without just complaining. And if she could hear something besides disappointment in your voice.

LEROY. She's learned to look down at me, Patty, you know that.

PATRICIA (*strongly, but nearly a threat of weeping*). Well I hope you're not blaming me for that.

LEROY (*he holds back, stands silent. Then puffs out his cheeks and blows, shaking his head with a defensive grin*). Not my day, I see.

PATRICIA. Maybe it could have been.

LEROY. I was looking forward to telling you something.

PATRICIA. What.

LEROY. I got Harrelson to agree to twelve-thousand-five for the altar.

PATRICIA. There, you see – and you were so glad to accept eight! I told you . . . !

LEROY. I give you all the credit. I finally got it through my thick skull, I said to myself, okay, you are slower than most, but quality's got a right to be slow. And he didn't make a peep – twelve thousand, five hundred dollars.

She looks at him, immensely sad.

– Well why do you look so sad?

PATRICIA. Come here.

Draws him down, kisses him.

I'm glad . . . I started to think of all these years wasted trying to get you to charge enough, but I've decided to keep looking straight ahead, not back – I'm very glad you got the twelve. You've done a wonderful thing.

LEROY (*excited*). Listen, what has he got you on?

PATRICIA. Well I'm still a long way from perfect, but I . . .

LEROY. Patty, nothing's perfect except a hot bath.

PATRICIA. It's nothing to joke about. I told you I'm nervous, I'm not used to . . . to . . .

LEROY. He changed your medication, didn't he?

PATRICIA. I just don't want you to think I have no problems any more.

LEROY. Oh, I'd never think that, Patty. Has he put you on something new?

PATRICIA. *He* hasn't done anything.

Pause.

LEROY. Okay, I'll shut up.

She sweeps her hair back; he silently observes her. Then . . .

. . . This Mr Frick handles oil burners; I don't know if I can trust him but he says he'd give me a good buy. We could use a new burner.

PATRICIA. What would you say if I said I'm thinking of coming home.

LEROY (*a pause filled with doubt*). You are? When?

PATRICIA. Maybe next Thursday. For good.

LEROY. Uh-huh.

PATRICIA. You don't sound very positive.

LEROY. You know you're the only one can make that decision, Pat. You want to come home I'm always happy to take you home.

Slight pause.

PATRICIA. I feel if I could look ahead just the right amount I'd be all right.

LEROY. What do you mean?

PATRICIA. I realized something lately; when I'm home I have a tendency – especially in the afternoons when everybody's out and I'm alone – I look very far ahead. What I should do is only look ahead a little bit, like to the evening or the next day. And then it's all right. It's when I start looking years ahead . . .

Slight pause.

You once told me why you think I got sick. I've forgotten . . . what did you say?

LEROY. What do I really know about it, Pat?

PATRICIA. Why do you keep putting yourself down? – you've got to stop imitating your father. There are things you know very well. – Remind me what you said . . . Why am I sick?

LEROY. I always thought it was your family –

PATRICIA (*fingers pressing on her eyes*). I want to concentrate. Go on.

LEROY. They were so close, they were all over each other, and you all had this – you know – very high opinion of yourselves; each and every one of you was automatically going to go to the head of the line just because your name was Sorgenson. And life isn't that way, so you got sick.

Long pause; she stares, nodding.

PATRICIA. You've had no life at all have you.

LEROY. I wouldn't say that.

PATRICIA. I can't understand how I never saw it.

LEROY. Why? – it's been great watching the kids growing up; and I've had some jobs I've enjoyed . . .

PATRICIA. But not your wife.

LEROY. It's a long time since I blamed you, Pat. It's your upbringing.

PATRICIA. Well I could blame yours too, couldn't I?

LEROY. You sure could.

PATRICIA. I mean this constant optimism is very irritating when you're fifty times more depressed than I am.

LEROY. Now Patty, you know that's not . . .

PATRICIA. You are depressed, Leroy! Because you're scared

of people, you really don't trust anyone, and that's incidentally why you never made any money. You could have set the
world on fire but you can't bear to work along with other
human beings.

LEROY. The last human being I took on to help me tried to
steal my half-inch Stanley chisel.

PATRICIA. You mean you *think* he tried . . .

LEROY. I didn't think anything, I found it in his toolbox. And
that's an original Stanley, not the junk they sell today.

PATRICIA. So what!

LEROY. So what? – that man has three grandchildren! And
he's a Chapman – that's one of the oldest upstanding
families in the county.

PATRICIA (*emphatically, her point proved*). Which is why you're
depressed.

LEROY (*laughs*). I'm not, but why shouldn't I be? – a Chapman
stealing a chisel? I mean God almighty, they've had generals
in that family, secretaries of state or some goddam thing.
Anyway, if I'm depressed it's from something that happened, not something I imagine.

PATRICIA. I feel like a log that keeps bumping against another
log in the middle of the river.

LEROY. Boy, you're a real roller-coaster. We were doing great
there for a minute, what got us off on this?

PATRICIA. I can't be at peace when I know you are full of
denial, and that's saying it straight.

LEROY. What denial? – (*Laughs.*) You want me to say I'm a
failure?

PATRICIA. That is not what I . . .

LEROY. Hey, I know what – I'll get a bumper sticker printed up
– 'The driver of this car is a failure!' – I betcha I could sell a
hundred million of them . . . (*A sudden fury.*) . . . Or maybe I
should just drive out on a tractor and shoot myself!

PATRICIA That's a terrible thing to say to me, Leroy!

LEROY Well I'm sorry, Patty, but I'm not as dumb as I look –
I'll never win if I have to compete against your brothers!

PATRICIA (*chastened for the moment*). I did not say you're a failure.

LEROY. I didn't mean to yell; I'm sorry. I know you don't mean to sound like you do, sometimes.

PATRICIA (*unable to retrieve . . .*). I said nothing about a failure. (*On the verge of weeping.*)

LEROY. It's okay, maybe I am a failure; but in my opinion no more than the rest of this country.

PATRICIA. What happened? – I thought this visit started off so nicely.

LEROY. Maybe you're not used to being so alert; you've been so lethargic for a long time, you know.

She moves; he watches her.

I'm sure of it, Pat, if you could only find two ounces of trust I know we could still have a life.

PATRICIA. I know.

Slight pause; she downs tears.

What did you have in mind, exactly, when you said it was my upbringing?

LEROY. I don't know . . . I had a flash of your father, that time long ago when we were sitting on your porch . . . we were getting things ready for our wedding . . . And right in front of you he turns to me cool as a cucumber and says, (*Through laughter, mimicking Swedish accent.*) 'No Yankee will ever be good enough for a Swedish girl.' I nearly fell off into the rose bushes.

PATRICIA (*laughs with a certain delight*). Well, he was old fashioned . . .

LEROY (*laughing*). Yeah, a real old fashioned welcome into the family!

PATRICIA. Well, the Yankees *were* terrible to us.

LEROY. That's a hundred years ago. Pat.

PATRICIA (*starting to anger*). You shouldn't keep denying this! – They paid them fifty cents a week and called us dumb

Swedes with strong backs and weak minds and did nothing
but make us ridiculous.

LEROY. But Patty, if you walk around town today there isn't a
good piece of property that isn't owned by Swedes.

PATRICIA. But that's now.

LEROY. Well when are we living?

PATRICIA. We were treated like animals, some Yankee doctors
wouldn't come out to a Swedish home to deliver a baby . . .

LEROY (*laughs*). Well, all I hope is that I'm the last Yankee so
people can start living today instead of a hundred years ago.

PATRICIA. There was something else you said. About standing
on line.

LEROY. On line?

PATRICIA. That you'll always be at the head of the line
because . . . (*Breaks off.*)

LEROY. I'm the only one on it.

PATRICIA. . . . is that really true? You do compete, don't you?
You must, at least in your mind?

LEROY. Only with myself. We're really all on a one-person
line, Pat. I learned that in these years.

Pause. She stares ahead.

PATRICIA. That's very beautiful. Where'd you get that idea?

LEROY. I guess I made it up, I don't know. It's up to you, Pat –
if you feel you're ready, let's go home. Now or Thursday or
whenever. What about medication?

PATRICIA (*makes herself ready*). I wasn't going to tell you for
another week or two, till I'm absolutely rock-sure; – I've
stopped taking anything for . . . this is twenty-one days.

LEROY. *Anything?* (*She nods with a certain suspense.*) My God,
Patty. And you feel all right?

PATRICIA. . . . I haven't felt this way in – fifteen years. I've no
idea why, but I forgot to take anything, and I slept right
through till morning, and I woke up and it was like . . . I'd
been blessed during the night. And I haven't had anything
since.

LEROY. Did I tell you or didn't I!

PATRICIA. But it's different for you. You're not addictive . . .

LEROY. But didn't I tell you all that stuff is poison? I'm just flying, Patty.

PATRICIA (*clasps her hands to steady herself*). But I'm afraid about coming home. I don't know if I'm jumping the gun. I *feel* I could, but . . .

LEROY. Well let's talk about it. Is it a question of trusting yourself? Because I think if you've come this far . . .

PATRICIA. Be quiet a minute! (*She holds his hand.*) Why have you stayed with me?

LEROY (*laughs*). God knows!

PATRICIA. I've been very bad to you sometimes, Leroy, I really see that now. (*Starting to weep.*) Tell me the truth; in all these years, have you gone to other women? I wouldn't blame you, I just want to know.

LEROY. Well, I've thought of it but I never did anything.

PATRICIA (*looking deeply into his eyes*). You really haven't, have you?

LEROY. No.

PATRICIA. Why?

LEROY. I just kept hoping you'd come out of this.

PATRICIA. But it's been so long.

LEROY. I know.

PATRICIA. Even when I'd . . . throw things at you?

LEROY. Uh-uh.

PATRICIA. Like that time with the roast?

LEROY. Well, that's one time I came pretty close. But I knew it was those damned pills, not you.

PATRICIA. But why would you be gone night after night? That was a woman, wasn't it?

LEROY. No. Some nights I went over to the library basement to practice banjo with Phil Palumbo. Or to Manny's Diner for some donuts and talk to the fellas.

PATRICIA (*slightest tinge of suspicion*). There are fellas there at *night*?

LEROY. Sure; working guys, mostly young single fellas. But some with wives. You know – have a beer, watch TV.

PATRICIA. And women?

LEROY (*a short beat*). – You know, Pat – and I'm not criticizing – but wouldn't it be better for you to try believing a person instead of trying not to believe?

PATRICIA. I'm just wondering if you know . . . there's lots of women would love having you. But you probably don't know that, do you?

LEROY. Sure I do.

PATRICIA. You know lots of women would love to have you?

LEROY. . . . Well, yes, I know that.

PATRICIA. Really. How do you know that?

LEROY (*his quick, open laugh*). I can tell.

PATRICIA. Then what's keeping you? Why don't you move out?

LEROY. Pat, you're torturing me.

PATRICIA. I'm trying to find myself!

She moves in stress, warding off an explosion. There is angry resentment in his voice.

LEROY. I'd remember you happy and loving – that's what kept me; as long ago as that is now, I'd remember how you'd pull on your stockings and get a little make-up on and pin up your hair . . . When you're positive about life there's just nobody like you. Nobody. Not in life, not in the movies, not on TV.

Slight pause.

But I'm not going to deny it – if it wasn't for the kids I probably *would* have gone.

She is silent, but loaded with something unspoken.

You're wanting to tell me something, aren't you?

PATRICIA. . . . I know what a lucky woman I've been.

LEROY (*he observes her*). –What is it, you want me to stop

coming to see you for a while? Please tell me, Pat; there's something on your mind.

Pause. She forces it out.

PATRICIA. I know I shouldn't feel this way, but I'm not too sure I could stand it, knowing that it's never going to . . . I mean will it ever change any more?

LEROY. You mean – is it ever going to be 'wonderful'.

She looks at him, estimating.

Well – no, I guess this is pretty much it; although to me it's already wonderful – I mean the kids, and there are some clear New England mornings when you want to drink the air and the sunshine.

PATRICIA. You can make more out of a change in temperature than any human being I ever heard of – I can't live on weather!

LEROY. Pat we're getting old! This is just about as rich and handsome as I'm ever going to be and as good as you're ever going to look, so you want to be with me or not?

PATRICIA. I don't want to fool either of us . . . I can't bear it when you can't pay the bills . . .

LEROY. But I'm a carpenter – this is probably the way it's been for carpenters since they built Noah's ark. What do you want to do?

PATRICIA. I'm honestly not sure I could hold up. Not when I hear your sadness all the time and your eyes are full of disappointment. You seem . . . (*Breaks off.*)

LEROY. . . . How do I seem?

PATRICIA. I shouldn't say it . . .

LEROY. . . . Beaten. Like it's all gone by.

She doesn't contradict.

(*Hurt, but holding on*). All right, Patty, then I might as well say it – I don't think you *ever* had a medical problem; you have an attitude problem . . .

PATRICIA. My problem is spiritual.

LEROY. Okay, I don't mind calling it spiritual.

PATRICIA. Well that's a new note; I thought these ministers were all quacks.

LEROY. Not at all; but the ones who make house calls with women, eating up all the ice cream are not my idea of spiritual.

PATRICIA. *You* know what spiritual is?

LEROY. For me? Sure. Ice skating.

PATRICIA. Ice skating is spiritual?

LEROY. Yes, and skiing! To me spiritual is whatever makes me forget myself and feel happy to be alive. Like even a well-sharpened saw, or a perfect compound joint.

PATRICIA. Maybe this is why we can't get along – spiritual is nothing you can see, Leroy.

LEROY. Really! Then why didn't God make everything invisible! We are in this world and you're going to have to find some way to love it!

Her eyes are filling with tears.

Pounding on me is not going to change anything to wonderful, Patty.

She seems to be receiving him.

I'll say it again, because it's the only thing that's kept me from going crazy – you just have to love this world.

He comes to her, takes her hand.

Come home. Maybe it'll take a while but I really believe you can make it.

Uncertainty filling her face . . .

All right, don't decide now, I'll come back Thursday and we'll see then.

PATRICIA. Where are you going now?

LEROY. For my banjo lesson. I'm learning a new number. – I'll play it for you if you want to hear it.

PATRICIA (*hesitates, then kisses him*). Couldn't you do it on guitar?

LEROY. It's not the same on guitar.

He goes to his banjo case and opens it.

PATRICIA. But banjo sounds so picky.

LEROY. But that's what's good about it, it's clean, like a toothpick . . .

Enter the Fricks.

LEROY. Oh hi, Mrs Frick.

KAREN. He brought my costume. Would you care to see it? – (*To* FRICK.) This is her – Mrs Hamilton.

FRICK. Oh! How do you do?

KAREN. This is my husband.

PATRICIA. How do you do?

FRICK. She's been telling me all about you.

PATRICIA. Really? What for?

FRICK. Well what she says you've been telling her. About her attitude and all.

KAREN (*to* PATRICIA). Would you like to see my costume? I also have a blue one but . . .

FRICK (*overriding her*). . . . By the way, I'm Frick Lumber, I recognized your husband right away . . .

KAREN. Should I put it on?

PATRICIA. Sure, put it on!

LEROY starts tuning his banjo.

FRICK (*to* PATRICIA). All it is is a high hat and shorts, y'know . . . nothing much to it.

KAREN (*to* FRICK). Shouldn't I?

PATRICIA. Why not, for Heaven's sake?

FRICK. Go ahead, if they want to see it. (*Laughs to* PATRICIA.) She found it in a catalogue. I think it's kinda silly at her age, but I admit I'm a conservative kind of person . . .

KAREN (*cutting him off, deeply embarrassed*). I'll only be a minute. (*She starts out, and stops, and to* PATRICIA.) You really think I should?

PATRICIA. Of course!

FRICK (*suppressing an angry embarrassment*). Karen, honey, if you're going to do it, do it.

KAREN *exits with valise.* LEROY *tunes his instrument.*

FRICK. The slightest decision, she's got to worry it into the ground. – But I have to tell you, it's years since I've seen this much life in her, she's like day and night. What exactly'd you say to her? (*To* LEROY, *thumbing toward* PATRICIA.) She says she just opened up her eyes.

LEROY (*surprised*). Patricia?

FRICK. I have to admit, it took me a while to realize it's a sickness . . .

PATRICIA. You're not the only one.

FRICK. Looked to me like she was just favoring herself; I mean the woman has everything, what right has she got to start shooting blanks like that? I happen to be a great believer in self-discipline, started from down below sea level myself, sixty acres of rocks and swampland is all we had. That's why I'm so glad that somebody's talked to her with your attitude.

PATRICIA (*vamping for time*). What . . . what attitude do you mean?

FRICK. Just that you're so . . . so positive. (LEROY *looks up at* PATRICIA *thunderstruck.*) She says you made her realize all the things she could be doing instead of mooning around all day . . .

PATRICIA. Well I think being positive is the only way.

FRICK. That's just what I tell her . . .

PATRICIA. But you have to be careful not to sound so disappointed in her.

FRICK. I sound disappointed?

PATRICIA. In a way, I think. – she's got to feel treasured, you see.

FRICK. I appreciate that, but the woman can stand in one place for half an hour at a time practically without moving.

PATRICIA. Well that's the sickness, you see.

FRICK. I realize that. But she won't even go shopping.

PATRICIA. You see? You're sounding disappointed in her.

FRICK (*angering*). I am not disappointed in her! I'm just telling you the situation!

PATRICIA. Mr Frick, she's standing under a mountain a mile high – you've got to help her over it. That woman has very big possibilities!

FRICK. Think so?

PATRICIA. Absolutely.

FRICK. I hope you're right. (*To* LEROY, *indicating* PATTY.) You don't mind my saying it, you could do with a little of her optimism.

LEROY (*turns from* PATRICIA, *astonished*). Huh?

FRICK (*to* PATRICIA, *warmly*). Y'know, she made me have a little platform built down the cellar, with a big full-length mirror so she could see herself dance.

PATRICIA. But do you spend time watching her . . .

FRICK. Well she says not to till she's good at it.

PATRICIA. That's because she's terrified of your criticism.

FRICK. But I haven't made any criticism.

PATRICIA. But do you like tapdancing?

FRICK. Well I don't know, I never thought about it one way or another.

PATRICIA. Well that's the thing, you see. It happens to mean a great deal to her. . . .

FRICK. I'm for it, I don't mean I'm not for it. But don't tell me you think it's normal for a woman her age to be getting out of bed two, three in the morning and start practicing.

PATRICIA. Well maybe she's trying to get you interested in it. Are you?

FRICK. In tapdancing? Truthfully, no.

PATRICIA. Well there you go . . .

FRICK. Well we've got a lot of new competition in our fuel oil business. . . .

PATRICIA. Fuel oil!

FRICK. I've got seven trucks on the road that I've got to keep busy . . .

PATRICIA. Well there you go, maybe that's why your wife is in here.

FRICK (*visibly angering*). Well, I can't be waked up at two o'clock in the morning and be any good next day, now can I. She's not normal.

PATRICIA. Normal! They've got whole universities debating what's normal. Who knows what's normal, Mr Frick?

FRICK. You mean getting out of bed at two o'clock in the morning and putting on a pair of tap shoes is a common occurrence in this country? I don't think so. – But I didn't mean to argue when you're . . . not feeling well.

PATRICIA. I've never felt better.

She turns away, and FRICK *looks with bewildered surprise to* LEROY, *who returns him a look of suppressed laughter.*

FRICK. You sure know how to turn somebody inside out.

KAREN *enters; she is dressed in satin shorts, a tailcoat, a high hat, tap shoes, and as they turn to look at her, she pulls out a collapsible walking stick, and strikes a theatrical pose.*

PATRICIA. Well now, don't you look great!

KAREN (*desperate for reassurance*). You really like it?

LEROY. That looks terrific!

PATRICIA. Do a step!

KAREN. I don't have my tape. (*Turns to* FRICK, *timorously.*) But if you'd sing 'Swanee River . . .'

FRICK. Oh Karen for God's sake!

PATRICIA. I can sing it . . .

KAREN. He knows my speed. Please, John . . . just for a minute.

FRICK. All right, go ahead. (*Unhappily, he sings.*) 'Way down
upon the Swanee River . . .'
KAREN. Wait, you're too fast . . .
FRICK (*slower and angering*).
'Way – down – upon – the – Swanee River,
Far, far away.
That's where my heart is turning ever . . .'
(*Etc.*)

KAREN *taps out her number, laboriously but for a short stretch
with a promise of grace.* FRICK *continues singing . . .*

PATRICIA. Isn't she wonderful?
LEROY. Hey, she's great.

KAREN *dances a bit more boldly, a joyous freedom starting into
her.*

PATRICIA. She's marvellous! Look at her, Mr Frick.

A hint of the sensuous in KAREN *now:* FRICK, *embarrassed,
uneasily avoids more than a glance at his wife.*

FRICK. '. . . everywhere I roam . . .'
PATRICIA. Will you look at her!
FRICK (*hard-pressed, explodes*). I am looking at her, goddammit!

*This astonishing furious shout, his reddened face, stops everything.
A look of fear is on* KAREN's *face.*

KAREN (*apologetically to* PATRICIA). He was looking at me . . .
(*To* FRICK.) She didn't mean you weren't looking, she
meant . . .
FRICK (*rigidly repressing his anger and embarrassment*). I've got to
run along now.
KAREN. I'm so sorry, John, but she . . .
FRICK (*rigidly*). Nothing to be sorry about, dear. Very nice to
have met you folks.

He starts to exit. KAREN *moves to intercept him.*

KAREN. Oh John, I hope you're not . . . (going to be angry).

FRICK. I'm just fine. (He sees her despair coming on.) What are you looking so sad about? – you danced great . . . (She is immobile.) I'm sorry to've raised my voice but it don't mean I'm disappointed, dear. You understand? (A nervous glance toward PATRICIA. Stiffly, with enormous effort . . .) You . . . you danced better than I ever saw you. (She doesn't change.) Now look here, Karen, I hope you don't feel I'm . . . disappointed or something, you hear . . . ? Cause I'm not. And that's definite. (She keeps staring at him.) I'll try to make it again on Friday. – Keep it up.

He abruptly turns and exits.

KAREN stands perfectly still, staring at nothing.

PATRICIA. Karen?

KAREN seems not to hear, standing there facing the empty door in her high hat and costume.

How about Leroy playing it for you? (To LEROY.) Play it.

LEROY. I could on the guitar, but I never did on this . . .

PATRICIA. Well couldn't you try it? – I don't know what *good* that thing is.

LEROY. Well here . . . let me see.

He picks out Swanee River on banjo, but KAREN doesn't move.

PATRICIA. There you go, Karen! Try it, I love your dancing! Come on . . . (sings.) 'Way down upon the Swanee River . . .'

KAREN now breaks her motionlessly depressed mode and looks at PATRICIA. LEROY continues playing, humming along with it. His picking is getting more accurate . . .

PATRICIA. Is it the right tempo? Tell him!

KAREN (very very softly). Could you a little faster?

LEROY speeds it up. With an unrelieved sadness, KAREN goes into her number, does a few steps, but stops. LEROY gradually stops playing. KAREN walks out. PATRICIA starts to follow her but gives it up and comes to a halt.

LEROY turns to PATRICIA, who is staring ahead. Now she turns to LEROY.

He meets her gaze, his face filled with inquiry. He comes to her and stands there.

For a long moment neither of them moves. Then she reaches out and touches his face — there is a muted gratitude in her gesture.

She goes to a closet and takes a small overnight bag to the bed and puts her things into it.

LEROY watches her for a moment, then stows his banjo in its case, and stands waiting for her. She starts to put on a light coat. He comes and helps her into it.

Her face is charged with her struggle against her self-doubt.

LEROY (*laughs, but about to weep*). Ready?
PATRICIA (*filling up*). Leroy . . .
LEROY. One day at a time, Pat — you're already twenty-one ahead. Kids are going to be so happy to have you home.
PATRICIA. I can't believe it . . . I've had nothing.
LEROY. It's a miracle.
PATRICIA. Thank you.

Breaking through her own resistance, she draws him to her and kisses him. Grinning tauntingly . . .

That car going to get us home?
LEROY (*laughs*). Stop picking on that car, it's all checked out!

They start towards the door, he carrying her bag and his banjo.

PATRICIA. Once you believe in something you just never know when to stop, do you?

LEROY. Well there's very little rust, and the new ones aren't half as well-built . . .

PATRICIA. Waste not want not.

LEROY. Well I really don't *go* for those new Chevies . . .

She walks out, he behind her. Their voices are heard . . .

PATRICIA. Between the banjo and that car I've certainly got a whole lot to look forward to.

His laughter sounds down the corridor.

The PATIENT *on the bed remains motionless. A stillness envelops the whole stage, immobility seems eternal.*

End

The Ride Down
Mount Morgan

To Inge

The Ride Down Mount Morgan was first presented by Robert Fox at Wyndham's Theatre, London on 11 October 1991, with the following cast:

LYMAN FELT	Tom Conti
THEO FELT	Gemma Jones
LEAH FELT	Clare Higgins
BESSIE	Deirdre Strath
FATHER	Harry Landis
NURSE LOGAN	Marsha Hunt
TOM WILSON	Manning Redwood

Directed by Michael Blakemore
Designed by Tanya McCallin
Music by Barrington Pheloung
Sound by Paul Arditti

ACT ONE

Fleeting chords of music accompany the shifts of time and place.

A hospital bed with LYMAN FELT *in it. In a moment* NURSE LOGAN *enters. She is black. He is deeply asleep, snoring intermittently. His head and torso are covered with bandages, one leg is raised in a cast and one arm at an odd angle. She adjusts the mattress with a turn of a crank, then sits nearby and opens a magazine and idly turns pages, looking at photos. After a moment . . .*

LYMAN (*his eyes still shut*). Thank you, thank you all very much. Please be seated.

NURSE *turns, looks towards him.*

We have a lot of material . . . not material . . . yes, material . . . to cover this afternoon, so please take your seats and cross your legs. No-no . . . (*Laughs weakly.*) Not cross your legs, just take your seats . . .

NURSE. That was a lot of surgery, Mr Felt. You're supposed to be resting . . . Or you out?

LYMAN (*for a moment he sleeps, snores, then*). Today I'd like you to consider life insurance from a different perspective. I want you to look at the whole economic system as one enormous tit.

NURSE. Well, now! (*Embarrassed laugh.*)

LYMAN. So the job of the individual is to get a good place in line for a suck. Which incidentally gives us the word 'suckcess'. Or . . . or not. (*Snores deeply.*)

NURSE. You keep this up we're going to have to see about another shot . . . (*Goes back to turning pages.*)

FATHER *enters; wears a Panama hat, carries a cane, smokes a cigarette in a holder, drags a broad black cloth behind him. He comes and bends over* LYMAN *as though to kiss him . . .*

LYMAN *stiffens, utters a cry of mixed fear and hopeful surprise, his eyes still shut.*

FATHER *straightens up and shakes his head mournfully.*

FATHER. Very bad for business.

LYMAN *whimpers pleadingly.*

What you need skates for, you fall down they laugh at you. Never talk business with women, God only makes them for one thing, obey God. Your teeth stick out, ears stick out, everything stickin' out, I'm sorry to say you very stupid boy, big disappointment. (*Shaking his head he moves into darkness.*) Very bad for business.

LYMAN. I promise. Papa! (*Calling.*) I promise! (*He opens his eyes, gradually taking in the* NURSE.) You black?

NURSE. That's what they keep telling me.

LYMAN. You ah . . . RSP?

NURSE. RN? – Yes.

LYMAN. Good for you. I've got a big training programme for you guys, biggest in the industry, and first one to put you in sales. There's no election now, is there? Eisenhower or something?

NURSE. Eisenhower! He's long, long gone. And it's December.

LYMAN. Oh. 'Cause you're more likely to be talking to strangers election time . . . why can't I move, do you mind?

NURSE. You broke some bones. They say you went skiing down that Mount Morgan in a Porsche.

She chuckles. He squints, trying to orient himself.

LYMAN. What's that music? Sounds like Earl Hines.

NURSE. Music? There's no music.

LYMAN (*sings*). 'I'm just breezin' along with the breeze . . .' Listen to that, will you? . . . that just beautiful? (*Whistles the tune for a moment, then falls fast asleep again. Wakes.*) Still have some black friends. Say I'm a nigger underneath. (*Chuckle.*) That's an honour. Jimmy Baldwin liked my stories, when I was still a writer. Long time ago. (*Slight pause.*) My wife used to ski like a Methodist – straight up . . . she used to say I ski'd like an Arab – pants kept falling down. No chairlifts in those days, y'know – used to climb back up the mountain on your skis. Herringbone. Women did it easier 'cause their knees opened wider. Get horny just watching them climb. What'd you say?

NURSE. I didn't.

LYMAN. Oh. And where is this I am?

NURSE. Clearhaven Memorial Hospital.

LYMAN (*it is slowly penetrating*). *Clearhaven?*

NURSE. Your wife and daughter just arrived up from New York.

LYMAN (*canniness attempt, but still confused*) . . . From *New York?* Kinda looking woman, how old?

NURSE. Fifties, probably.

LYMAN (*alarm starts*). Who called them?

NURSE. What do you mean? Why not?

LYMAN. And where is this?

NURSE. Clearhaven. – I'm from Canada myself, I just started here. We've still got railroads in Canada.

LYMAN. Listen . . . I'm not feeling well. What are we talking about Canadian railroads for?

NURSE. No, I just mentioned it as there is a storm.

LYMAN. Now what . . . what . . . what was that about my wife from New York?

NURSE. She's here in the waiting room. And your daughter.

LYMAN (*peering intensely*). – And this is *where?*

NURSE. I told you, Clearhaven Memorial.

LYMAN (*looks around warily*). You have a mirror?

NURSE. Mirror? Sure. (*Takes one out of her purse, goes to him.*) You don't look extra great, I can tell you that now.

LYMAN (*looks at himself, touches bandage in surprise*). Could you . . . touch me? (*She puts finger on his cheek. He lowers the mirror, looks at her, suddenly angry.*) Who the hell called them, for God's sake?

NURSE. I'm new here! I'm sorry if I'm not satisfactory. (*Unnerved, she returns to her chair.*)

LYMAN (*high anxiety*). Who said you're not satisfactory? What's all this unnecessary . . . *verbiage?* – Not verbiage, for Christ's sake, I meant . . . (*Panting.*) Listen, I absolutely can't see anyone and they have to go back to New York right away.

NURSE. But as long as you're awake . . .

LYMAN. Immediately! Get them out of here, okay? (*Stab of pain.*) Oh! – Listen . . . there's nobody else, is there? To see me?

NURSE. Not that I noticed.

LYMAN. Please, quickly, go – I can't see anybody!

Bewildered, she exits.

LYMAN. My God, how could I have done this! – Christ, I can just see them! . . . Oh how terrible! It can't happen, it mustn't happen!

Slipping out from the rear of the cast, he moves into the clear – still in hospital gown, but not bandaged. The empty cast remains on the bed as it was. His eyes wide as he stares at his catastrophic vision . . .

Oh, I can just see it . . . Bessie is weeping, oh poor darling! But not Theo . . . No, Theo is completely controlled, yes . . . controlled and strong . . .

As he speaks the beds move away behind him, and a chintz-covered wicker chair and couch, furniture of the hospital waiting room, truck on. Lights change to brighter, more cheerful tone. His wife, THEODORA *and daughter,* BESSIE, *are seated on the couch.*

No-no, it mustn't happen . . . !

He is looking on in high tension, but since he is invisible to the others he may move right up to them, sit beside them, etc.

THEODORA'S *beaver coat is beside her;* BESSIE'S *cloth coat on her lap.* THEODORA *is sipping a cup of tea. She is an idealistic, intellectually forceful woman turning fifty now, physically strong, if somewhat stiff and ungainly.*

BESSIE, *after a moment, is suddenly swept by a fit of sobbing, and covers her face.* THEODORA *grips her hand.*

THEO. Darling, you must try not to.

BESSIE. I can't help it.

THEO. Of course you can. Try to think of all the happiness; think of his laughter; Daddy loves life, he'll fight for it.

LYMAN (*looking on admiringly*). God, what a woman!

BESSIE . . . I guess I've just never had anything really bad happen.

LYMAN. Oh, my dear Bessie . . . !

THEO. But you'll see as you get older – everything ultimately fits together . . . and for the good.

LYMAN (*a mix of love and condescension toward her naivety*). Ah, bless her, what an American!

THEO. – Now come, Bessie. – Remember what a wonderful time we had in Africa? Think of Africa.

BESSIE. What an amazing woman you are, Mother.

NURSE LOGAN *enters*.

NURSE. It'll still be a while before he can see anybody. There's a good motel just up the highway; it's ski season but my husband can probably get you in, he ploughs their driveway.

BESSIE. Do you know if he's out of danger?

NURSE. I think so but I'm sure the doctors will let you know. (*Obviously changing subject.*) I can't believe you made it up from New York in this sleet.

THEO. One does what one has to. – I think I would like to lie down, would you call the motel? It was a terrible drive. . . .

NURSE. Sometimes I feel like going back to Canada – at least we had a railroad.

THEO. We'll have them again; things may take time in this country but in the end we get them done.

NURSE *exits*.

THEO (*turns to* BESSIE, *smiling painfully*). What was so funny?

BESSIE (*touching her mother's hand*). It's nothing . . .

THEO. Well, what was it?

BESSIE. Well, I mean . . . things really don't always get done in this country.

THEO (*disengaging her hand; she is hurt*). I think they do, ultimately. I've lived through changes that were inconceivable thirty years ago. (*Straining to laugh.*) I'm really not *that* naive, Bessie.

BESSIE (*angering*). Well, don't be so upset, it's not important. (*Pause. To heal things . . .*) – They certainly are very nice people around here, aren't they?

THEO. Oh yes. I've often been sorry you never knew small-town life, there *is* a goodness.

BESSIE. I'm wondering if we ought to call Grandma Esther.

THEO. If you like. (*Slight pause.*) She gets so impressively emotional, that's all.

BESSIE. Well I won't if it upsets you.

THEO. Oh, no, I have nothing against her any more; she simply never liked me and I always knew it, that was all. But she loves you.

BESSIE. I know she's a superficial woman, but she can really be so funny and . . .

THEO. Funny, yes.

BESSIE. I've never understood why you feel she's cold.

THEO. I just don't like women who are forever seducing their sons.

LYMAN (*with mock-righteousness*). Right!

THEO. It's a miracle she didn't turn him into a homosexual.

LYMAN. Perfect!

THEO. I used to think it was because he didn't marry a Jew.

BESSIE. But she didn't either.

THEO. What she does never counts, dear. But you go ahead, call her, she is his mother and she adores you.

LEAH enters. *She is about thirty; blondined hair, in an open racoon coat, high heels.* NURSE *enters with her.*

LYMAN (*on the instant she enters, claps hands over his eyes*). No, she mustn't! It can't happen! It mustn't! (*Unable to bear it he starts to flee, but stops as . . .*)

LEAH. After all the money we've put into this hospital it

seems to me I ought to be able to speak to the Chief Nurse, for Christ's sake!

NURSE. I'm doing my best to get her for you . . . !

LEAH. Okay, I'll wait here. (NURSE *starts to go*.) I'm only asking for a little information, dear!

NURSE *exits. Pause.*

LEAH *sits, but quickly stands again and moves restlessly.* THEO *and* BESSIE *observe her indirectly, with polite curiosity. Now their eyes meet. She throws up her hands.*

The same thing when I had my baby here, it was like pulling teeth to get them to tell me if it was a boy or a girl.

BESSIE. Is it an emergency?

LEAH. My husband; he cracked up the car on Mount Morgan. You?

BESSIE. My father. It was a car, too.

LYMAN. Oh dear God, not this way . . . please!

THEO. The roads are impossible.

LEAH. It's that damned Mount Morgan road – there've been half a dozen horrible crashes in the last couple of years . . . I still can't believe it – the man driving on ice . . . and at night yet! It's incomprehensible! (*A sudden explosion.*) Damn them, I have a right to know what's happening! (*She charges out.*)

BESSIE. Poor thing.

THEO. But she *knows* how busy they are . . .

Silence now; THEO *leans back, closing her eyes. Another sobbing fit threatens* BESSIE *who downs it, covers her eyes. Then suddenly she breaks down and weeps.*

Oh, Bessie, dear, try not to . . .

LYMAN (*staring front*). . . . if I could only get myself over to the window . . . and out!

BESSIE (*shaking her head helplessly*). . . . I just love him so!

LEAH returns, more subdued now. She sits tiredly, closes her eyes. Pause. She gets up, goes to a window, looks out.

LEAH. Will you look at that moon? Everybody smashes up in the dark and now you could read a paper out there.

BESSIE. You live around here?

LEAH. Not far. We're on the lake.

BESSIE. It looks like such beautiful country.

LEAH. Oh yes. But I'll take New York any time. (*A great sob bursts from her.*) I'm sorry.

She weeps helplessly into her handkerchief. BESSIE is affected and begins weeping, too.

THEO. Now really . . . ! (*Shakes BESSIE's arm.*) Stop this!

She sees LEAH's indignant look.

You still don't know how serious it is, do you? Why are you carrying on like this?

LEAH (*rather unwillingly*). You're probably right.

THEO (*exulting – to BESSIE as well*). Of course! I mean there's always time to despair, why should . . . ?

LEAH (*sharply*). I *said* you were right, I was agreeing with you!

THEO goes stiff, turns slightly away.

I'm sorry.

Short pause.

LYMAN. What admirable women! What strong, definite characters. Now what would they say next?

BESSIE. You raise things on your place?

LEAH. We grow most of what we eat. We have sixty head of cattle. And we're starting to raise thoroughbreds now, in a small way.

BESSIE. Oh, I'd love that . . .

LEAH. I envy your calmness – both of you. Really, you've made me feel better. What part of New York are you in?

BESSIE. East 74th Street.

LYMAN (*gripping his head*). Oh no! No-no . . . !

LEAH. 74th, really? We often stay at the Carlyle. . . .

BESSIE. Oh, it's very near.

THEO. You sound like a New Yorker.

LEAH. I went to NYU School of Business for three years, and I really love the city, but I was raised here in Elmira and my business is here, so . . . (*She shrugs. Goes to the window again.*)

THEO. What sort of business do you have?

LEAH. Insurance.

LYMAN (*hitting his head*). No! – that's enough, stop it!

BESSIE. Oh, that's what Daddy does!

LYMAN (*hands clasped, facing heaven*). Oh don't, don't let it happen!

LEAH. Well, there's a million of us. You in it, too?

BESSIE. No, I'm at home . . . take care of my husband.

LEAH. I'm hoping to sell out, in maybe three–four years, get a place in New York and just paint morning to night the rest of my life.

BESSIE. Really? – My husband's a painter.

LEAH. Professionally or . . . ?

BESSIE. Oh yes. He's Harold Lamb.

LYMAN. No! – My God!

He rushes out holding his head.

LEAH. Harold Lamb?

LYMAN *returns, unable not to witness this.*

LEAH *has ceased all movement, staring at* BESSIE. *Now she turns to stare at* THEODORA.

THEO. What is it?

LEAH. Your husband is really Harold Lamb?

BESSIE (*very pleased and proud*). You've heard of him?

LEAH (*to* THEO). You're not Mrs Felt, are you?

THEO. Why, yes.

LEAH (*her puzzled look*). Then you . . . (*Breaks off, then . . .*) You're not here for Lyman, are you?

BESSIE. You know Daddy?

LEAH. But . . . (*Turning from one to the other.*) How'd they come to notify *you*?

THEO (*uncomprehending, but beginning to take affront*). What's that?

LEAH. Well . . . after so many years.

THEO. What do you mean?

LEAH. But it's over nine . . .

BESSIE. What is?

LEAH. Your divorce.

THEO *and* BESSIE *are struck dumb. A silence.*

You're Theodora Felt, right?

THEO. Who *are* you?

LEAH. I'm Leah. Leah Felt.

THEO (*a haughtiness begins*). Felt!

LEAH. Lyman is my husband.

THEO. Who *are* you? What are you talking about!

BESSIE (*intensely curious about* LEAH, *she angers at* THEO). Well, don't get so *angry*, for heaven's sake!

THEO. Be quiet!!

LEAH (*seeing* THEO's *genuineness*). Well, you're divorced, aren't you?

THEO. Divorced! – Who the hell *are* you!

LEAH. I'm Lyman's wife.

THEO *sees she is a serious woman; it silences her.*

BESSIE. When . . . when did you . . . ? I mean . . .

THEO (*in motion again*). She's insane! – She's some kind of a nut!

LEAH (*to* BESSIE). It'll be nine years in September.

THEO. And who performed this . . . this *event*?

LEAH. The Elmira City Hall Clerk, and then a Rabbi the next day. My son's name is Benjamin, for his mother's father, and Alexander for Lyman's father – Benjamin Alexander Felt.

THEO (*with a weak attempt to sustain mockery*). Really!

LEAH. Yes. I'm terribly sorry if you didn't know.

THEO. Didn't know *what*? What are you *talking* about?

LEAH. We have been married over nine years, Mrs Felt.

THEO. Have you! And I suppose you have some document . . . ?

LEAH. I have our marriage certificate, I guess . . .

THEO. You guess!

LEAH (*angrily*). Well I'm sure I do! And I know I have Lyman's will in our safe deposit box . . .

THEO (*helplessly mocking*). And it names you as his wife!

LEAH. And Benjamin his son.

THEO *is halted by her factuality.*

. . . But I guess you have more or less the same . . . is that right?

THEO *is still as a stone.*

There was really no divorce?

BESSIE (*with a glance at her stricken mother . . . softly, almost apologetically*). . . . No.

LEAH. Well, I think we'd better . . . meet, or something. And talk, Mrs Felt? I understand your feelings, but you'll just have to believe it, I guess: – we have a terrible problem. Mrs Felt?

THEO. It's impossible; nine years ago . . . (*To* BESSIE.) that's when we all went to Africa.

BESSIE. Oh, right! – the safari!

THEO (*to* LEAH, *with a victorious, if nearly demented laugh*). We were never closer in our lives! We travelled through Kenya, Nigeria . . . (*As though this clinched everything.*) . . . we even flew to Egypt!

NURSE *enters. It instantly galvanizes all of them. She glances from one to the other.*

NURSE. Doctor Lowry would like to see Mrs Felt now.

For one instant no one moves – then both THEO *and* LEAH *rise simultaneously. This actualization of* LEAH's *claim stiffens* THEO, *forcing her to start assertively toward the* NURSE — *and she sways and starts to fall to the floor.*

LEAH. Catch her!
BESSIE. Mother!

NURSE *and* BESSIE *catch* THEO, *then lower her to the floor.* LEAH *becomes frantic through this collapse, rushing toward the periphery, yelling . . .*

LEAH. Help here, someone's fainted! Where's a doctor, goddamit!

Blackout.

Two upholstered chairs. LEAH *is seated facing* TOM WILSON, *a middle-aged but very fit lawyer who is reading a will, and sipping coffee. After a moment she gets up and moves to a point and stares, eyes filled with fear. Then, dialling a phone, turns to him.*

LEAH. — Sorry I'm not being much of a hostess. Sure you wouldn't like some toast?
TOM (*immersed*). Thanks. I'm just about done here.
LEAH (*dialling*). God, I dread it — my boy'll be home from school any minute . . . (*In phone.*) Put my brother on, Tina. . . . Lou? — I don't know, they won't let me see him yet. What'd Uniroyal say? *What?* Well, call L.A. this minute! I want that business! — But we discussed all this yesterday! Jetlag doesn't last this long. (*Hangs up.*) I don't know what it is; there's no sense of continuity from one day to another any more.

TOM *closes the file.*

I know you're her lawyer, but I'm not really asking advice, am I?

TOM. I can discuss this. (*Returning her the file.*) The will does recognize the boy as his son but you are not his wife.
LEAH (*lifting the file*). But this refers to me as his wife . . .

TOM. That's meaningless – he never divorced. However . . . (*Breaks off, pressing his eyes.*) I'm just stunned, I can't absorb it.

LEAH. I'm still in mid-air some place.

TOM. What'd you ask me? Oh yes – provided the legal wife gets a minimum of one third of the estate he can leave you as much as he likes. So you're very well taken care of. (*Sighs. Leans forward gripping his head.*) He actually flies a plane, you say?

LEAH. Oh yes, soaring planes too. We own one.

TOM. You know, for years he never got off the ground unless it was unavoidable.

LEAH. Oh, he's wonderful in the air. (*Pause.*) I'm not here. I'm simply . . . not here. Can he be insane?

TOM. . . . May I ask you . . . ?

LEAH. Please. . . . Incidentally, have you known him long?

TOM. Sixteen, seventeen years. – When you decided to marry, I assume he told you he'd gotten a divorce . . .

LEAH. Of course. We went to Reno together.

TOM. No kidding! And what happened?

LEAH. God, I'd forgotten all about this . . . (*Breaks off.*) How could I have been so *stupid*! – You see, it was July, a hundred and ten on the street, so he had me stay in the hotel with the baby while he went to the court to pick up his divorce decree . . . (*She goes silent.*)

TOM. Yes?

LEAH (*shaking her head*). It's incredible . . . I was curious to see what a decree looked like . . .

LYMAN *enters, wearing short-sleeved summer shirt.*

no particular reason, but I'd never seen one . . .

LYMAN. I threw it away.

LEAH (*a surprised laugh*). Why?

LYMAN. I don't want to look back. Darling, I feel twenty-five! Come, I have a car and driver downstairs. Are you ready for your wedding? (*Laughs.*) You look stunned!

LEAH (*kisses him lightly*). I never really believed you'd do it, darling.

LYMAN. I wouldn't have believed it either . . .

He sits with her, TOM *a foot or two away.*

There's some primitive connection between us, Leah –
your smell, maybe – something that goes down to the
depths of my brain. I think of you with another man and
I get nauseous.

Pause.

LEAH. I never thought you could commit to a woman.

LYMAN. Maybe I got too old to keep changing beds any
more. – But I think it's also that . . . see, I've been very
successful, but it was really an accident that I got into
business, and it turned out to be a false direction. The
only reality to me is still poetry, the words; everything
else is smoke blowing away. – I know I'll never write
any more – that bird won't sing on a diet of money –
but I just can't go on faking emotions. And with you I
feel like a rock in the river, you flow around me easy and
slow . . . You feel committed, don't you?

LEAH. Yes, absolutely. But can I tell you the wedding vow
I wish we could make? – It's going to sound strange,
but . . .

LYMAN. No! – Say it!

LEAH. I'm embarrassed but I will; 'Dearly beloved, I
promise everything good, but I might have to lie to you
sometime'. Could one say that and still love someone?
Because it's the truth . . . nobody knows what can happen,
right?

LYMAN (*slight pause*). What balls you have to say that! Yes,
it's the truth and I love you for it!

He kisses her, then seems distracted.

LEAH. You seem drained – are you sorry you divorced
her?

LYMAN. I'm . . . a little scared, that's all, but it's natural.
– Tell you what. I'm going to learn to fly a plane . . .

LEAH. But you hate flying!

LYMAN (*lifts her to her feet*). Yes, but no more fear. Ever. Of any kind! – I'm going to fly! Now come to your wedding, Leah, my darling!

LYMAN *exits without lowering his arm. She turns to* TOM.

LEAH. . . . And it was all lies! How is it possible! Why did he do it? What did he want?

TOM. Actually . . . (*Tries to recall.*) . . . You know . . . I think we did have a discussion about a divorce . . .

LEAH. You did? When?

TOM. About nine years ago . . . although at the time I didn't take it all that seriously. He suddenly popped in to my office one day with this 'research' he said he'd done . . .

LYMAN *enters in a business suit.*

LYMAN. . . . I've been looking into bigamy, Tom.

TOM (*laughs, surprised*). Bigamy! – What are you talking about?

LYMAN. There was a piece in the paper a few weeks ago. There's an enormous amount of bigamy in the United States now.

TOM. Oh? But what's the point . . . ?

LYMAN. I've been wondering – how about bigamy insurance? Might call it the Desertion Protection Plan.

TOM (*laughs*). It's a great name for a policy . . . but you're kidding.

LYMAN. I mean this. We could set the premiums very low, like a few cents a week. Be great, especially for minority women.

TOM. Say now! – (*Greatly admiring.*) Where the hell do you get these ideas!

LYMAN. I don't think they're ideas, I just try to put myself in other people's places. (*Laughs, enjoying his immodesty.*) – It's what made me what I am today! Incidentally, how frequently do they prosecute for bigamy any more, you have any idea?

TOM. No. But it's a victimless crime so it can't be often.

LYMAN. That's my impression, too. Get somebody to research it, will you, I want to be sure. – I'll be in Elmira till Friday. (*Starts to leave but dawdles.*)

TOM. Why do I think you're depressed?

LYMAN. Slightly, maybe. (*The self-deprecating grin.*) I'm turning forty-seven this July.

TOM. Fifty's much tougher, I think.

LYMAN. My father died at fifty-seven.

TOM. Well, anyway, you're in better shape than anybody I know.

LYMAN. Famous last words.

TOM. – Something wrong, Lyman?

LYMAN (*slight pause; he decides to tell*). I was having lunch today at the Four Seasons, and just as I'm getting up this woman – beautifully dressed, smile on her face, cool as a cadaver – leans over me and says, 'I hope you drop dead you son of a bitch'. You know what she was talking about.

TOM. I can't believe that's still happening.

LYMAN. Oh, three or four times a year; they don't always come out with it but I can see it in their eyes. But it's okay . . .

TOM. You sure you're not imagining it?

LYMAN. No-no, people still think I turned in my partner to save myself. – Which maybe I did, but I don't think so, I think Raoul paid for his crookedness, period. But I'll always be contemptible to a lot of people, Tom. – I still love that guy, though – we had some great years together building the firm. . . . Well, what the hell, that's life. (*Short pause.*) – This is why you were so against my testimony, isn't it?

TOM. You have a barbed wire conscience, Lyman. I knew how close you were and I thought it would come back to bother you.

LYMAN. I might have lost Theo if I'd gone to jail.

TOM. Well, it's over the dam and out to sea.

LYMAN. I did the right thing; it's just the imputation of

cowardice that . . . (*Breaks off.*) Well, fuck it, I've lived my life and I refuse to be ashamed of it! Talk to you soon. (*Stands, but hesitates to leave.*)

TOM. – Is there something else?

LYMAN. I don't think I have the balls.

A pause. LYMAN *stands perfectly still, controlled; then, facing his challenge, turns rather abruptly to* TOM.

It's funny about you, Tom – I've been a lot closer to other men, but there's nobody I trust like you. (*A grin.*) I guess you know I've cheated on Theodora, don't you?

TOM. Well, I've had my suspicions, yes – ever since I walked in on you humping that Pakistani typist on your desk.

LYMAN (*laughs*). 'Humping'! – I love that Presbyterian jive of yours, haven't heard that in years.

TOM. Quaker.

LYMAN (*confessionally, quietly*). I don't want to be that way any more. It's kind of ridiculous at my age, for one thing. (*With difficulty.*) I think I've fallen in love.

TOM. Oh, don't tell me!

LYMAN (*pointing at him and laughing*). Look at you! – God, you really love Theodora, don't you!

TOM. Of course I do! – You're not thinking of divorce, are you?

LYMAN. I don't know what I'm thinking. It's years since anything like this has happened to me. But I probably won't do anything . . . maybe I just wanted to say it out loud to somebody.

TOM. I have a feeling it'll pass.

LYMAN. I've been waiting for it to, but it keeps getting worse. – I've frankly never believed monogamous guys like you are honestly happy, but with her I can almost see it for myself. And that can't ever be with Theodora. With her I'll be on the run till I croak, and that's the truth.

TOM. You know she loves you deeply. Profoundly, Lyman.

LYMAN. Tom, I love her too, but our neuroses just don't match.

TOM. Frankly, I can't imagine you apart from each other
– you seem so dependent.

LYMAN. I know. I've always relied on her sense of reality,
especially her insights into this country. But I just don't
want to cheat any more – it's gotten hateful to me, all
deception has. It's become my Nazi, my worst horror –
I want to wear my own face on my face every day till I
die. Or do you think that kind of honesty is possible?

TOM. I don't have to tell you, the problem is not honesty
but how much you hurt others with it.

LYMAN. Right. What about your religion – ? But there's
no solution there either, I guess.

TOM. I somehow can't imagine you praying, Lyman.

Short pause.

LYMAN. Is there an answer?

TOM. I don't know, maybe all one can do is hope to end
up with the right regrets.

LYMAN (*silent a moment*). You ever cheated, Tom?

TOM. No.

LYMAN. Honest to God? – I've seen you eye the girls
around here.

TOM. It's the truth.

LYMAN. Is that the regret you end up with?

TOM *laughs bashfully. Then* LYMAN *joins him. And suddenly,
his suffering is on his face.*

. . . Shit, that was cruel, Tom, forgive me, will you?
– Dammit, why do I let myself get depressed? It's all
pointless guilt, that's all! Here I start from nothing, create
forty-two hundred jobs for people and raise over sixty
ghetto blacks to office positions when that was not easy
to do – I should be proud of myself, son of a bitch! And
I am! I am!

He bangs on the desk, then subsides, looks front and downward.

I love your view. That red river of tail-lights gliding down
Park Avenue on a winter's night – and all those silky white

thighs crossing inside those heated limousines . . . Christ, can there be a sexier vision in the world?

Turning back to TOM.

I keep thinking of my father – how connected he was to his life; couldn't wait to open the store every morning and happily count the olives, rearrange the pickle barrels. People like that knew the main thing. Which is what? What's the main thing, do you know?

TOM *is silent.*

– Look, don't worry, I really can't imagine myself without Theodora, she's a great, great wife! . . . I love that woman! It's always good talking to you, Tom.

Starts to go; halts.

Maybe it's simply that if you try to live according to your real desires, you have to end up looking like a shit. (*He exits.*)

LEAH *covers her face and there is a pause as* TOM *observes her.*

TOM. I'm sorry.
LEAH. He had it all carefully worked out from the very beginning.
TOM. I'd say it was more like . . . a continuous improvisation.
LEAH. What's so bewildering is that he was the one who was pushing to get married, not me . . .

LYMAN *hurries on in a winter overcoat, claps a hand over her mouth.*

LYMAN. Don't tell me it's too late. (*Kisses her.*) Did you do it?
LEAH. I was just walking out the door for the hospital.
LYMAN. Oh, thank God. (*Draws her to a seat, and pulls her down.*) Please, dear, give me one full minute and then you can do as you like.

LEAH. Don't, Lyme, it's impossible. (*Obviously changing the subject – with pain.*) – Listen, up here they're all saying Reagan's just about won it.

LYMAN. Well, he'll probably be good for business. The knuckle heads usually are. – You know if you do this it's going to change it between us.

LEAH. Darling, it comes down to being a single parent and I just don't want that.

LYMAN. I've already named him.

LEAH (*amused, touching his face*). How do you know it's a him?

LYMAN. I'm never wrong, I have a very intimate relationship with ladies' bellies. His name is Benjamin after my mother's father who I loved a lot, and Alexander after my father. (*Grins at his own egoism.*) You can put in a middle name.

LEAH (*an unhappy laugh*). Well, thanks so much! (*Tries to stand up but he holds her.*) He asked me not to be late.

LYMAN. The Russians – this is an ancient custom – before an important parting, they sit for a moment in silence. Give Benjamin this moment.

LEAH. He is not Benjamin, now stop it!

LYMAN. Believe in your feelings, Leah, the rest is nonsense. Reach into yourself; what do you really and truly want? (*Silence for a moment.*) I would drive him to school in the mornings, take him to ball games.

LEAH. Twice a month?

LYMAN. With the new office set up here, I could easily be with you more than half the time.

LEAH. And Theodora?

LYMAN. It's difficult to talk about her.

LEAH. With me, you mean.

LYMAN. I can't lie to myself, darling, she's been a tremendous wife. It would be too unjust.

LEAH. But keeping it secret – where does that leave me? It's hard enough to identify myself as it is. And I can't believe she won't find out sooner or later, and then what?

LYMAN. If I actually have to choose it'll be you. But she

doesn't know a soul in this whole area, it'd be a million to one shot for her ever to find out. I'm practically with you half the time now, and it's been pretty good, hasn't it?

LEAH (*touching her belly*). . . . But what do we tell this . . . ?

LYMAN. . . . Benjamin.

LEAH. Oh stop calling him Benjamin! It's not even three weeks!

LYMAN. That's long enough to be Benjamin – he has a horoscope, stars and planets; he has a *future*!

LEAH. There's something . . . why do I feel we're circling around something? There's something I don't believe here – what is it?

LYMAN. Maybe that I'm this desperate. (*Kisses her belly.*)

LEAH. Are you? – I can't express it . . . there's just something about this baby that doesn't seem . . . I don't know – *inevitable*.

LYMAN. Darling, I haven't wanted anything this much since my twenties, when I was struggling to be a poet and make something of my own that would last.

LEAH. Really.

LYMAN. It's the truth.

LEAH. That's touching, Lyman. . . . I'm very moved.

So it is up in the air for the moment.

But I can't, I won't. It's the story of my life, I always end up with all the responsibility; I'd have to be in total charge of your child and I know I'd resent it finally – and maybe even you as well. You're putting me back to being twelve or thirteen and my parents asking *me* where to go on vacations, or what kind of car to buy or what colour drapes. I hate that position! One of the most sensuous things about you was that I could lie back and let you drive, and now you're putting me behind the wheel again. It's just all wrong.

LYMAN. But when you're thirty-six I'll be sixty.

LEAH. Doesn't mean a thing to me.

LYMAN. Dummy, you're not listening; when you're forty-six I'll be *seventy*.

LEAH. Well it's not eighty. – I've made up my mind, dear.

LYMAN. I thought if we lived together let's say ten years, you'd still be in the prime, and pretty rich, and I'd . . .

LEAH. . . . Walk away into the sunset?

LYMAN. I'm trying to be as cruelly realistic as life, darling. Have you ever loved a man the way you love me?

LEAH. No.

LYMAN. Well? That's the only reality.

LEAH. You can drive me to the hospital, if you like realism so much.

She stands. He does.

You look so sad! You poor man . . .

She kisses him; a silent farewell is in this kiss; she gets her coat and turns to him.

– I won't weaken on this, dear, so make up your mind.

LYMAN. We're going to lose each other if you do this. I feel it.

LEAH. Well, there's a very simple way not to lose me, dear, I guess that's why they invented it. – Come, wait in the hospital if you want to. If not, I'll be back tomorrow. (*She draws him on, but he halts.*)

LYMAN. Will you give me a week to tell her? It's still early for you, isn't it?

LEAH. Tell her what?

LYMAN. . . . That I'm going to marry you.

TOM. I see.

LYMAN moves into darkness.

LEAH. I don't understand it; he'd had dozens of women, why did he pick me to be irreplaceable? (*Looks down at her watch, stares in silence.*) God! – how do I tell my boy?

TOM. He's nine now?

LEAH. And worships Lyman. Worships him.

TOM. I'd better get to the hospital. (*He moves to go, halts hesitantly.*) Don't answer this if you'd rather not, but you think you could ever take him back?

LEAH (*thinks for a moment*). How can you possibly ask me that? It's outrageous.

TOM. I'm terribly sorry. I apologize.

LEAH (*curiosity aroused*). – Why? – Would Theodora?

TOM. I've no idea.

LEAH. Why do you ask me?

TOM. I've a feeling it could be important.

LEAH. It's impossible. How could I trust him again? (*Slight pause.*) She struck me as a rather judgemental sort of woman . . . is she?

TOM. Oh, she has a tender side too. – I guess she hasn't had time to think of the future, any more than you have.

LEAH (*slight pause*). – I could never take him back, but all this reminds me of an idea I used to have about him that . . . well, it'll sound mystical and silly . . .

TOM. Please. I'd love to understand him.

LEAH. Well . . . it's that he *wants* so much; like a kid at a fair; a jelly apple here, a cotton candy there, and then a ride on a loop-the-loop . . . and it never lets up in him; and sometimes it almost seemed as though he'd lived once before, another life that was completely deprived, and this time around he mustn't miss a single thing. And that's what's so attractive about him – to women, I mean – Lyman's mind is up your skirt but it's such a rare thing to be wanted like that – indifference is what most men feel now – I mean they have appetite but not hunger – and here is such a splendidly hungry man and it's simply . . . well . . . precious once you're past twenty-five. I tell you the truth, somewhere deep down I think I sensed something about him wasn't on the level, but . . . I guess I must have loved him so much that I . . . (*Breaks off.*) – But I mustn't talk this way; he's unforgiveable! It's the rottenest thing I've ever heard of! The answer is no, absolutely not!

TOM (*nods, thinks, then . . .*). Well, I'll be off. I hope it's not too difficult for you with the little boy.

He exits.

Blackout on LEAH.

LYMAN *is softly snoring; a troubled sleep, however – bad dreams.*

FATHER *appears, smoker's cough announces him in the surrounding dimness.*

FATHER. Stay off the roof – very bad for business the way you fucking all these girls up there. Why you talking so much to your mother? – she don't know nothing. She don't want to go Florida with me, she says one state is enough. Stupid woman. I thought a Jewish woman gonna be smart. You both a big disappointment to me. I'm telling you stay off the roof before you make disgrace for the business.

TOM *enters with* NURSE. *She raises* LYMAN'S *eyelid.* FATHER *disappears, coughing.*

NURSE. He still goes in and out but you can try him.
TOM. Lyman? Can you hear me?

LYMAN *stops snoring but eyes remain shut.*

It's Tom Wilson.
NURSE. Keep going, he shouldn't be staying under this much by now.
LYMAN (*opens his eyes*). *You* in the store?
TOM. It's the hospital.
LYMAN. Hospital . . . ? Oh Jesus, right, right . . . (*Trying to focus.*) Give me a second, a little mixed up . . . How'd you get here?
TOM. Theodora called me.

LYMAN. Theodora?

TOM. Your car is registered in the city so the State Police called her.

LYMAN. I had some weird dream that she and Bessie . . . (*Breaks off.*) They're not here, are they?

NURSE. I told you your wife came . . .

TOM (*to* NURSE). Excuse us, please?

NURSE. But I told him.

She exits.

TOM. They've met, Lyman.

LYMAN. Theo . . . didn't collapse, did she?

TOM. Yes, but she's come around, she'll be all right.

LYMAN. I don't understand it, I think I dreamed the whole thing . . .

TOM. Well, that wouldn't be too difficult, it's all pretty inevitable.

LYMAN. Why're you sounding so brutal?

TOM. There's no time to fool around, you've got things to decide. It's all over television . . .

LYMAN. Oh no, dammit! – Have you met her? – Leah?

TOM. We've had a talk. She's a considerable woman.

LYMAN. Isn't she? – She's furious, too, huh?

TOM. Well, what do you expect?

LYMAN. See . . . I thought I'd somehow divorce Theo later. – But it sort of settled in where I had both of them. And after a while it didn't seem so God-awful . . . What about Bessie? –

TOM. It's hit her pretty bad, I guess.

LYMAN. God, and poor little Benny! Jesus, if I could go through the ceiling and just disappear!

TOM. It's all over the television. I think you ought to issue a press statement to cut the whole thing short. As to your intentions.

LYMAN. What intentions? Just give each of them whatever they want. I'll probably go and live somewhere . . . maybe like Brazil or something . . .

TOM. You won't try to hold onto either of them?

LYMAN. They wouldn't have anything to do with me. My God . . . (*He turns away, tears in his eyes.*) How could I have destroyed everything like this! (*Higher intensity.*) Why did I drive into that storm! – I can't understand it! I had the room in Howard Johnson's, I think I was even in bed . . .

TOM. Maybe it'll clear up. – Can you give Theo a few minutes? She wants to say goodbye.

LYMAN. How can I face her? Ask her to wait till tomorrow, maybe I'll feel a little better and . . .

THEODORA and BESSIE enter; LYMAN does not see them as they are above him.

TOM. They're here, Lyman.

LYMAN closes his eyes, breathing fast. BESSIE, holding THEODORA by the elbow, accompanies her to the bedside.

BESSIE (*whispering in some shock*). Look at his bandages! (*Turning away.*) Oh, Mother!

THEO. Stop that.

Bending to LYMAN.

Lyman?

He can't get himself to speak.

It's Theodora.

LYMAN (*opening his eyes.*) Hi.

THEO. How are you feeling?

LYMAN. Not too bad now. I hope I make sense with all this pain killer . . . Is that you, Bessie?

BESSIE. I'm only here because of Mother.

LYMAN. Oh. Okay. I'm sorry, Bess – I mean that my character's so bad. But I'm proud that you have enough strength to despise me.

BESSIE. But who wouldn't?

LYMAN. Good! – (*His voice starts to break but he controls himself.*) That was well-spoken, Sweety.

BESSIE (*with quick anger*). Don't call me that . . .

THEO (*to* BESSIE). Sshh! (*She has been observing him in silence.*) Lyman? – Is it true?

He closes his eyes.

I have to hear it from you. Did you marry that woman?

Deep snores emerge from the head bandage.

THEO (*more urgently*). Lyman?

BESSIE (*points*). He's not really sleeping!

THEO. Did you have a child with that woman? Lyman? I insist!!

LYMAN *emerges from behind the upstage head of the bed, hands clapped to his ears, while the bandaged figure remains as it was. He is in a hospital gown, but unbandaged.*

Light change; an ethereal colourlessness now, air devoid of pigment.

LYMAN (*agonized cry, ears still covered*). I hear you!

THEO *continues to address the cast's bandaged head, and* BESSIE *is fixed on it as well, but her attitude has become formalized as she too becomes a part of his vision – everything is now super-emphatically threatening to him.*

THEO. What in God's name have you done!

Almost writhing in conflict LYMAN *clears his throat. He remains upstage of the bed.*

BESSIE (*bent over the head of the cast*). Ssh! He's saying something!

LYMAN. I realize . . . how crazy it sounds, Theodora . . . (*Breaks off.*)

THEO. Yes?

LYMAN. . . . . I'm not really sure, but . . . I wonder if this crash . . . was maybe to sort of subconsciously . . . get you both to . . . meet one another, finally.

THEO (*with disgust*). Meet *her*?

LYMAN. I know it sounds absurd but . . .

THEO. Absurd! – It's disgusting! She's exactly the type who forgets to wash out her panties.

LYMAN (*wincing; but with a certain pleasurable recognition*). I *knew* you'd say that! – I admit it, though, there *is* a sloppy side to her . . .

THEO. She's the worst generation in our history – screw anybody in pants, then drop their litters like cats, and spout mystic credos on cosmic responsibility, ecology and human rights!

LYMAN. To my dying day I will stand amazed at your ability to speak in complete paragraphs!

THEO. I insist you explain this to me yourself. Lyman? – Lyman!

LEAH *enters.* THEO *reacts instantly.*

There'll be no one in here but the family! (*To* BESSIE.) Get the nurse!

LEAH (*despite* THEO, *she approaches the cast, but with uncertainty about his reaction to her*). Lyman!

THEO (*to* TOM). Get her out of here!

TOM *is immobile, and she goes to him furiously.*

She does not belong here!

LEAH (*to the cast . . . with a certain warmth*). It's me, Lyme. Can you hear me?

THEO (*rushing threateningly toward* LEAH). Get out, get out, get out . . . !

Just as THEO *is about to lay hands on* LEAH, LYMAN *throws his arms up and cries out imploringly.*

LYMAN. I want everybody to lie down!

The three women instantly de-animate as though suddenly falling under the urgency of his control. LYMAN *gestures, without actually touching them, and causes* LEAH *and* THEO *to lie on the bed on which his cast remains.* BESSIE *looks on, motionless.*

LEAH (*as she lies down; voice soft, remote*). What am I going to tell Benny? Oh gee whiz, Lyman, why did you . . . ?

THEO (*lying down beside* LEAH). You have a bitter smell, you should use something.

LEAH. I have, but he likes it.

THEO. Blah. (*To* LYMAN.) And what would you say if one of us took another man to bed and asked you to lie next to him?

LYMAN (*lifting off her glasses*). Oh, I'd kill him, dear; but you're a lady, Theodora; the delicate sculpture of your noble eye, your girlish faith in me and your disillusion; your idealism and your unadmitted greed for wealth; the awkward tenderness of your wooden fingers, your incurably Protestant cooking; your *savoir faire* and your sexual inexperience; your sensible shoes and devoted motherhood, your intolerant former radicalism and stalwart love of country now – your Theodorism! Who can ever take your place!

LEAH (*laughing*). Why am I laughing!!

LYMAN. Because you're a fucking anarchist, my darling! (*He stretches out over both of them.*) Oh what pleasure, what intensity! Your counter currents are like bare live wires! (*Kisses each in turn.*) I'd have no problem defending both of you to the death! Oh the double heat of two blessed wives – this is heaven!

Rests his head on LEAH *while holding* THEO's *hand to his cheek.*

LEAH. Listen, you've got to make up your mind about something.

LYMAN. I'm only delaying as long as possible, let's delay it all till we die! Delay, delay, how delicious, my loving Leah, is delay!

THEO (*sits up*). How you can still go on talking about love is beyond my understanding.

LYMAN. And still I love you, Theodora, although certain parts of your body fill me with *rage*!

THEO. So you simply got yourself some other parts instead.

LEAH, *still lying on her back, raises one leg in the air, and her skirt slides down exposing her thigh.*

LYMAN (*replying to* THEODORA, *kissing* LEAH's *thigh*). That's the truth, yes – at least it was all flesh at first.

LEAH (*stretching out her arms and her body*). Oh how good that was! I'm still pulsing to the tips of my toes. (*Stands, comes up to him.*) You're really healthy, aren't you?

LYMAN (*wry attempt*). You mean for my age? – yes.

LEAH. I did *not* mean that!

He links arms and they walk; the others go dark while bright sunlight hits them.

LYMAN. My health is terrific; in fact, it keeps threatening my dignity.

They sit – as on a park bench.

LEAH. Why!

LYMAN. Well, how do I come to be lounging in a park with a girl, and on a working day! I really hadn't planned to do that this afternoon. Did you know I was going to?

LEAH. No . . . but I never do.

LYMAN. Really? But you seem so organized.

LEAH. In business; but not in pleasure.

LYMAN. What surprised me was the openness of your laughter with those heavy executives at the table.

LEAH. Well, your presentation was so funny. I'd heard you were a real brain, not a comic.

LYMAN. Well, insurance is basically comical, isn't it? – at least pathetic.

LEAH. Why?

LYMAN. You're buying immortality, aren't you? – Reaching up out of the grave to pay the bills, remind people of your love? It's poetry. The soul was once immortal, now we've got an insurance policy.

LEAH. You sound pretty cynical about it.

LYMAN. Not at all – I started as a writer, nobody lusts after the immortal like a writer.

LEAH. How'd you get into insurance?

LYMAN. Pure accident. How'd you?

LEAH. My mother had died, my dad had his stroke, and insurance was something I could do from home. Dad knew a lot of people, being a doctor, so the thing just took off.

LYMAN. Don't take this wrong – but you know what I find terrifically sexy about you?

LEAH. What?

LYMAN. Your financial independence. Horrible, huh?

LEAH. Why? – (*Wryly.*) Whatever helps, helps.

LYMAN. You don't sound married, are you?

LEAH. It's a hell of a time to ask! (*They laugh, come closer.*) I can't see myself getting married . . . not yet anyway. – Incidentally, have you been listening to me?

LYMAN. Yes, but my attention keeps wandering toward a warm and furry place . . .

She laughs, delighted.

It's funny; my generation got married to show its maturity, yours stays single for the same reason.

LEAH. That's good!

LYMAN. How happy I am! (*Sniffs his hands.*) . . . Sitting in Elmira in the sun with you, and your scent still on my hands! God! – all the different ways there are to try to be real!

LEAH. What do you mean by that?

LYMAN. I don't know the connection, but when I turned twenty I sold three poems to the *New Yorker* and a story to *Harper's*, and the first thing I bought was a successful blue suit to impress my father how real I was even though a writer. He ran an appetizer store on 40th Street and Ninth Avenue, Middle Eastern specialties . . . you know, olives, grape leaves . . . all kinds of wonderful-smelling realities. (*Grinning, near laughter.*) And he sees the suit and says, 'How much you pay?' And I said, 'Twenty-nine-fifty,' thinking I'd got a terrific bargain. And he says, 'Pray God keep an eye on you the rest of your life'.

LEAH (*laughs*). That's awful!

LYMAN. No! – It spurred me on. (*Laughs.*) He had two pieces of wisdom – never trust anybody, and never forgive. – Funny, it's like magic, I simply can't trace how we got into that bed.

LEAH (*a glance at her watch*). I really have to get back to the office. – But is Lyman an Albanian name?

LYMAN. Lyman's the judge's name in Wooster, Mass., who gave my father his citizenship. Felt is short for Feltman, my mother's name, because my father's was unpronounceable and they wanted a successful American for a son.

LEAH. Then your mother was Jewish.

LYMAN. And the source of all my conflicts. In the Jewish heart is a lawyer and a judge, in the Albanian a bandit defying the government with a knife.

LEAH. What a surprise you are! –

She stands, and he does.

LYMAN. Being so silly?

LEAH. Being so interesting, and in the insurance business.

LYMAN (*taking her hand*). When was the moment? – I'm just curious.

LEAH. I don't know . . . I guess at the conference table I suddenly thought, 'he's basically talking to me'. But then I figured, this is probably why he's such a great salesman, because everybody he talks to feels loved.

LYMAN. You know? – I've never before with a Jewish girl.

LEAH. Well, you're my first Albanian.

LYMAN. There's something venerable in your eyes. Not old – ancient. Like our people's.

LEAH (*touches his cheek*). Take care, dear.

LYMAN (*as she passes before him to leave he takes her hand*). Why do I feel I know nothing at all about you?

LEAH (*shrugs, smiles*). Maybe you weren't listening . . . which I don't mind if it's in a good cause.

LYMAN (*letting go her hand*). I walk in the valley of your thighs.

She laughs, gives him a quick kiss.

When you move away now, would you turn back to me for a moment?

LEAH (*amused*). Sure, why?

LYMAN (*half-kidding, his romanticism*). I have to take a small commuter plane and if I die I want that vision as I go down —

LEAH (*backing away with a wave*). Bye, Lyman. . . .

LYMAN. Can I ask who that fellow was banging on your apartment door?

LEAH (*caught off-guard*). Somebody I used to go with . . . he was angry, that's all.

LYMAN. Are you afraid of him?

LEAH (*shrugs in an accepted uncertainty*). See you, dear.

She turns and walks a few yards, then halts and turns her head to look back at him over her shoulder.

LYMAN. Beautiful.

She exits.

LYMAN (*alone*). Miraculous. (*Thinks for a moment.*) Still . . . was it really all *that* great? (*A phone is lit up, he goes to it, picks it up, troubled.*) Theo? — Hi, darling, I'm just about to take off. Oh, definitely, it has the makings of a much bigger operation; had a talk with Aetna's chief rep. here, and she's agreed to take us on, so I'll probably be spending more time here. — Yes, a woman; she's got a great agency, I might try to buy into her. — Listen, dear, how about you flying up here and we rent a car and drive through the Cherry Valley — it's all bursting into bloom now! — Oh, I forgot; no-no, you'd better go to your meeting then, it's okay; no, it just suddenly hit me how quickly it's all going by and . . . You ever have the feeling that you never got to really *know* anybody?

She never has; he resents it, and a sharpness enters his voice.

Well, yes, I do feel that sometimes, very much; I feel I'm going to vanish without a trace.

Unhappily now, hidden anger, the romance gone.

Theo, dear, it's nothing against you, I only meant that with all the analysis and the novels and the Freuds we're still as opaque and unknowable as some line of statues in a church wall.

He hangs up. Now light strikes the cast on the bed. He moves to it and looks down at himself. BESSIE, THEO *and* LEAH *are standing motionless around the bed and* TOM *is off to one side, observing.* LYMAN *slowly lifts his arms and raises his face like a supplicant.*

We're all in a cave . . .

The three women now begin to move, ever so slightly at first; their heads turning as they appear to be searching for the sight of something far away or overhead or on the floor.

. . . where we entered to make love or money or fame. It's dark in here, as dark as sleep, and each one moves blindly, searching for another; to touch, hoping to touch and afraid; and hoping, and afraid.

As he speaks the women and TOM *move in criss-crossing, serpentine paths, just missing one another, spreading out further and further across the stage until one by one they disappear.* LYMAN *has moved above the bed where his cast lies.*

Now that we're here . . . what are we going to say?

He bends and enters his cast.

Light change: pigment and the air of the present reality return.

TOM *appears with the* NURSE. *They come to the cast and she examines* LYMAN, *bending close to his face exactly as she did at her first entrance at the beginning of the scene, lifting his eyelid, etc.*

NURSE. He still goes in and out but you can try him. Come, dear, Doctor doesn't want you staying under too long.

TOM. Lyman? Theo wants to come in to say goodbye.

THEO enters with BESSIE and they come to the bed.

THEO. Lyman? Did you marry that woman? I insist you explain this to me yourself! I insist!

LEAH enters. THEO reacts instantly.

I'll have no one but the family in this room!

LEAH proceeds anyway.

Get out, get out, get out!

As she nears LEAH to strike her . . .

An animal outcry from LYMAN's very bowel. It stops THEO, and all turn to look at him as he lies there panting for breath. Now he turns to look at them all.

LYMAN. My God! – *again?*
THEO (*quietly to TOM, mystified*). What did he say?

ACT TWO

The hospital waiting room. TOM *seated with* THEODORA.

TOM. Really, Theo, I wish you'd let Bessie take you back to the city.

THEO. Please stop repeating that! (*Slight pause.*) I need to talk to him . . . I'll never see him again. I can't simply walk away. Is my head trembling?

TOM. A little, maybe. Should you let one of the doctors look at you?

THEO. I'll be all right, my family has a tendency to tremors, I've had it for years when I'm tense. What time is it?

TOM. Give them a few minutes more. – You seem pale.

THEO (*presses fingers against her temples to steady herself*). When you spoke with this woman . . . was there any feeling about . . . what she has in mind?

TOM. She's as much in shock as you. The child was her main concern.

THEO. Really. Somehow I wouldn't have thought so.

TOM. Oh, I think he means everything to her.

THEO (*begrudgingly*). Well, that's nice. – Messes like this are basically comical, aren't they – until you come to the children. I'm very worried about Bessie. She lies there staring at the ceiling. She can hardly talk without starting to weep. He's been her . . . her world. (*She begins to fill up.*) . . . You're right; I think I'll go. It just seemed unfinished, somehow . . . but maybe it's better to leave it this way . . . (*She starts for her bag, stops.*) I don't know what to do. One minute I could kill him, the next I wonder if some . . . aberration got into him . . .

LEAH *enters. They did not expect to see each other. A momentary pause.* LEAH *sits.*

LEAH. Good morning.

TOM. Good morning.

Awkward silence.

LEAH (*asking*). He's not in his room?

THEO (*difficult for her to address* LEAH, *turns to her only slowly*). They're treating his eye.

LEAH. His eye?

TOM. It's nothing serious, he tried to climb out his window during the night. Probably in his sleep. His eyelid was slightly scratched by a rhododendron.

THEO (*a stab at communication*). He must not have realized he's on the ground floor.

Short pause.

LEAH. Hm! That's interesting, because a friend of ours, Ted Colby, called last night – he's commander of the State Police here. They'd put up a wooden barrier across the Mount Morgan road when it got so icy; and he thinks Lyman moved the barrier aside.

TOM. How could they know it was him?

LEAH. There was only one set of tyre tracks in the snow.

THEO. Oh my God.

LEAH. He's worried about him. They're good friends, they go hunting together.

THEO. Lyman hunts?

LEAH. Oh, sure.

THEO *shakes her head incredulously.*

– But I can't imagine him in that kind of depression, can you?

TOM. Actually . . . yes, I think I can.

LEAH. Really. He's always seemed so . . . up with me, and happy.

THEO *glances at her, irked, then away.* LEAH *glances at her watch.*

I just have to settle some business with him for a few minutes. I won't be in your way.

THEO. *My* way? You're free to do anything you like, as far as I'm concerned.

LEAH (*slightly taken aback*). Yes . . . the same with me . . .

in your case. (*Beat.*) – I mean as far as I'm concerned. (*The hostility turns her to look at her wristwatch again.*) I want to tell you . . . I almost feel worse for you, somehow, than for myself.

THEO (*hard laugh*). Why! Do I seem *that* old?

The second rebuff stiffens LEAH.

I shouldn't have said that. I apologize. I'm exhausted.

LEAH (*letting it pass*). How is your daughter? – She still here?

THEO (*a hostile colour despite everything*). In the motel. She's devastated.

TOM. Your boy taking it all right?

LEAH. No, it's wracked him, it's terrible. (*To* THEO). I thought Lyman might have some idea how to deal with him, the kid's always idolized him so. I'm really at my wits' end.

THEO (*bitterly angry, but contained*). We are his dust; we billow up behind his steps and settle again when he passes by. Billie Holliday . . . (*She touches her forehead.*) I can't recall when she died, it's quite a while, isn't it?

TOM. Billie Holliday? Why?

TOM *and* LEAH *observe, puzzled, as* THEO *stares in silence. Then* . . .

LEAH. Why don't I come back in a couple of hours – I've got a nine o'clock conference call and it's getting a bit late . . . (*She stands, goes to* THEO, *and extending her hand.*) Well, if we don't meet again . . .

THEO (*briefly touching her hand, hostility momentarily overcome*). . . . . Do you understand this?

LEAH. It's baffling. He's raced the Mount Morgan road, he knows what it's like even in summer.

THEO. Raced? You mean cars?

LEAH. Sure. He has a Lotus and a Z. He had a Ferrari, but he totalled it . . .

THEO *turns and stares at space.*

I was thinking before . . .

THEO. He's always been terrified of speed; he never drives over sixty . . .

LEAH. . . . He reminds me of a frog . . .

THEO. A frog?

LEAH. . . . I mean you never know when you look at a frog whether it's the same one you just saw or a different one. (*To* TOM.) When you talk to him – the television is hounding us; he really has to make a definite statement to stop all this stupid speculation.

THEO. What speculation?

LEAH. You've seen the *Daily News*, haven't you?

THEO. What!

LEAH. We're both on the front page with a headline . . .

TOM (*to* THEO, *placating*). It's unimportant . . .

THEO (*to* LEAH). What's the headline?

LEAH. 'Who Gets Lyman?'

THEO. How dare they!

TOM. Don't be upset, I'll get a statement from him this morning . . .

LEAH. Goodbye, Mrs . . . (*Stops herself; a short laugh.*) I was going to call you Mrs Felt but . . . (*Correcting again.*) Well you are, aren't you – I guess I'm the one who's not! I'll come by about ten or so.

She exits.

THEO. She wants him back, doesn't she?

TOM. Why?

THEO (*a bitter little laugh*). Didn't you hear it? – She's the only one he was happy with!

TOM. Oh, I don't think she meant . . .

THEO (*fiercely*). That's *all* she meant; there's something vulgar about that woman. – I pity her, though – with such a young child. (*She fumes in silence.*) *Can* it have been suicide?

TOM. Frankly, in a way I'd almost hope so.

THEO. . . . It would indicate a moral conscience, is that what you mean?

TOM. Well, I'd hate to think all this duplicity meant nothing to him.

THEO. Unless his mind simply shattered. The Lyman I know could no more hunt animals and drive racing cars than . . .

TOM. I don't know, maybe he just wanted to change his life; do things he'd never done; be a completely different person . . .

THEO (*stares for a moment*). . . . Maybe not so different.

TOM. How do you mean?

THEO (*a long hesitation*). I don't know why I'm still trying to protect him – he tried to kill me once.

TOM. You're not serious.

LYMAN *appears in sunlight in swim trunks, inhaling deeply on a boat deck. She begins walking toward him.*

THEO. Oh yes! I didn't know this woman existed then, but I see now it was just about the time they had either married or were on the verge.

Moving toward LYMAN *her coat slides off, revealing herself in a swimsuit.*

He seemed very strange, unreal. We'd gone for a two-day sail off Montauk . . .

LYMAN *is doing breathing exercises.*

LYMAN. The morning mist rising from the sea is always like the first day of the world . . . the 'oysterygods and the visigods . . .'

THEO *enters into his acting area.*

THEO. *Finnegan's Wake*. Like some tea, dear?

LYMAN. Great! – yes!

Kneels, tuning a radio; static as she pours tea.

I'll get the weather. Is that a new suit? – It's sexy as hell.

THEO. Two years ago. You bought it for me in San Diego.

LYMAN (*mimes pistol to his head*). Bang.

ANNOUNCER (*voice over*). . . . Due to the unusually warm spring tides there've been reported shark sightings off Montauk . . . one is reported to be twelve to fourteen feet long . . .

Heavy static intervenes; he mimes switching radio off.

LYMAN. Jesus.

THEO. Oh, that's ridiculous, it's only May! I'm going in for a dip . . . (*She looks over into the ocean.*)

LYMAN. But the man said . . .

THEO. Nonsense. I've sailed around here since my childhood, and father did and grandfather – there are never sharks till July if at all, the water's much too cold. Come in with me?

LYMAN (*resentfully smiling*). I'm the Mediterranean type – we're unreliable and hate cold water. But go ahead, I'll wait here and admire you.

THEO. Darling, I'm allowed to say that sharks are impossible this time of year, aren't I?

LYMAN (*strained laugh at the outrageousness*). I know I shouldn't say this, Theo, but how you can hang onto your convictions in the face of a report like that . . . just seems . . . I don't know – fanatical.

THEO (*a hard, determined laugh*). Now that is really uncalled for! You're just as stubborn as I am when you're committed to something.

LYMAN. Goddamit, you're right! And I love your convictions! You're just great, honey – (*Swings an arm around her.*) go ahead, I'll keep an eye out.

THEO (*with loving laughter*). You simply can't stand me contradicting you, darling, but it's the best exercise for your character.

LYMAN (*laughs, with her, points front*). Right! And a miserable character it is. Into the ocean! (*He leaves her side, scans ocean.*)

THEO (*bends to dive*). On the mark . . . get set . . .

LYMAN (*points leftward*). What's that out there?

THEO. No, sharks always move, that's a log.

LYMAN. Okay, go ahead, jump in.

THEO. I'll run in! Wait, let me warm up. (*Backs up to make a run for it.*) Join me! – Come on.

LYMAN. I can't, dear, I fear death.

She is behind him, running in place. His back is to her and his eye now catches sight of something toward the right; his mouth drops open, eyes staring in horror following the moving shark. She bends to start her run.

THEO. Okay, one . . . and a two . . . and a . . . three!

She runs and as she comes abreast of him he suddenly reaches out and stops her at the edge.

LYMAN. Stop!

He points front; she looks, horror rising in her face as their eyes follow the fish.

THEO. My God, the *size* of him! Ahhh . . . !

She bursts into tears of released terror; he takes her into his arms.

LYMAN. Honey . . . when are you going to believe something I say!

THEO. Oh, I'm going to be sick . . . !

About to vomit, she bends and rushes into darkness. Light goes out on LYMAN and up on TOM in the waiting room; he is staring ahead, listening. The light widens and finds THEO standing in her fur coat.

TOM. That sounds like he saved you.

THEO. Yes, I've always tried to think of it that way, too, but I have to face everything now – (*Coming downstage; newly distressed by the memory.*) it was not quite the top of his voice. I mean it wasn't . . .

Light flares up on LYMAN in trunks and at top voice and horror, shouts . . .

LYMAN. Stop!!

He stands mesmerized looking at the shark below. Blackout on him.

THEO. . . . It was more like . . .

Light flares up on LYMAN *again, and merely semi-urgently – as he did in the scene.*

LYMAN. Stop.

Blackout LYMAN.

THEO. I tell you he was on the verge of letting me go.

TOM. You're angry now, Theo, I don't think you really believe that. I mean, how could you have gone on living with him?

THEO. Well, we did have two serious breakups and . . . months have gone by without – relations. (*An embarrassed, determined smile as she gradually becomes furious.*) – No, dammit, I'm not going to evade that question. – How I've gone on? Maybe I'm corrupt, Tom. I wasn't, once, but who knows, now? He's rich, isn't he? and vastly respected, and what would I do with myself alone? Why does anybody stay together, once they're realized who they're with? (*Suddenly livid.*) What the hell am I hanging around here for? This is the stupidest thing I've ever done in my life! (*Indignantly grabs her bag.*)

TOM. You love him, Theo. (*Physically stops her.*) Please go home, will you? And give it a few weeks before you decide anything? (*A silence. Then she stifles a sob as he embraces her.*) I know how crazy this sounds, but part of him worships you. I'm sure of it.

THEO (*suddenly screams into his face*). I hate him. *I hate him!*

She is rigid, pale, and he grips her shoulders to steady her. A pause.

– I must lie down. I just have to know what happened, as long as I'm here. We'll probably go back to the City by

noon. – Or maybe I'll just leave, I don't know. Call me
if he wakes up soon. (*She passes her hand across her brow.*)
– I feel I look strange.

TOM. Just tired. Come, I'll find you a cab . . .

THEO. It's only a few blocks, I need the air. (*Starting off,
turns back.*) How beautiful the country still is up here –
it's kind of surprising that it hasn't been ruined!

She exits.

Alone, TOM *stands staring into space, arms folded, trying to
figure an approach.*

Blackout.

LYMAN's *room. He is deeply asleep, snoring placidly at first.
Now there is a tensing up, he is groaning in his sleep.* LEAH
and THEODORA *appear on either side of him, but on elevated
platforms, like two stone deities; they are in kitchen aprons,
wifely ribbons tying up their hair.*

*But something menacing about their deathly stillness as the
sepulchral dream-light finds them, motionless in this tableau.
After a long moment they animate. As in life they are reserved,
each measuring herself against the other.*

*Notwithstanding the humour of some of their remarks, their
manner of speaking is godlike, deathly.*

THEO. I wouldn't mind at all if you did some of the cooking,
I'm not all that super.

LEAH (*generously*). I hear you make good desserts, though.

THEO. Apple cobbler, yes; gingerbread with whipped
cream. (*Gaining confidence.*) And exceptional waffles for
breakfast, with real maple syrup, although he's had to cut
out the sausages.

LEAH. I can do potato pancakes and szegedina goulash.

THEO (*disapproving*). And all that *paprika*?

LEAH. It has to be blended in, of course.

THEO (*at a loss, sensing a defeat*). Ah, blended in! I'm afraid I couldn't do something like that.

LEAH (*smiling, brutally pressing her advantage*). Oh yes, blended in and blended really *in*! And my gefulte fish is feather-light. (*Clapping her cupped palms together.*) I wet my hands and keep patting it and patting it till it shapes up just perfect!

THEO (*struggling with loss*). He does love my glazed ham. Yes – and my boiled tongue. (*A sudden bright idea.*) Custard!

LEAH (*generously*). You can do all the custard and glazed ham and I'll do all the gefulte fish and goulash . . . *and* the blending in.

THEO. But may I do *some*? Once or twice a month, perhaps?

LEAH. Let's leave it up to him – some months you can do more . . .

THEO. Yes! – and some months you.

LEAH. 'Kay! Would you wash out my pants?

THEO. Certainly. As long as he tells me my lies.

LEAH. Good! Then you'll have your lies and I'll have mine!

LEAH & THEO. Hurrah for the menu!

LEAH (*filled with admiration*). You certainly have class!

LYMAN *chuckles in his sleep as they come together downstage of the cast and embrace each other warmly; and arm in arm walk upstage to his bed. Each kneebends on opposite sides of the bed, resting her chin on the mattress and staring at him from both sides. He changes . . .*

He begins to pant in anxiety, as though imprisoned by their threatening stares. Now each gently but surely grasps one of his hands and sucks on one of his fingers. He writhes in terror, gasping for breath and shouting incoherently. The women stand and go into darkness.

A black cloth bundle, unobtrusive on the floor, stirs and he bends over the edge of the bed and looks down at it. From it a lighter flares, lighting a cigarette; FATHER *sits up and coughs quietly, then inhales the cigarette.*

FATHER. Stupid. Very bad for business.

LYMAN *slips out of the cast, picks up a broad-brimmed Panama hat from the floor and defiantly mimes urinating into it; then with a certain anticipation of violence offers it to* FATHER *who snatches it out of his hands angrily.*

FATHER (*looking into the hat*). What you do here?

LYMAN, *defiance weakening, looks into the hat and becomes intensely embarrassed and grips his crotch. Tries to get behind the bed, but* FATHER *stands and begins to stalk him, the broad black cloth trailing behind him.*

A rhythmic, profound sound as from the centre of the earth.

You piss in your father's hat, you son of a bitch? You Communist, something?

LYMAN. No-no, Pa! – Pumpkin pie!

FATHER. Pumpkin pie? You think you gonna be an American? *You? American?* You make me laugh? (*Looks into his hat.*) How I gonna tip my hat to the customers, full of piss? Very bad for business!

LYMAN (*hopefully enticing*). Fifty thousand dollars?

FATHER. And how you pay me back? More piss? (*Stands with the help of a walking stick, raises the cloth with both hands.*) All you can do? – Piss in your father's hat?! I catch you I show you something. . . !

He tries to throw the black cloth over LYMAN's *head.* LYMAN *skitters away . . .*

LYMAN. Don't, Pa, please. . . !

FATHER (*points with stick at* LYMAN's *penis*). Why everything on you sticks out?

LYMAN *climbs into his cast with little frightened cries,* FATHER *now starts viciously pounding the stick on the bed; with each blow a booming sound resonates as from deep in the earth . . .*

Stay off the roof with those American girls! All whores, these American girls! Very bad for business!

LYMAN is crying out in terror as the NURSE hurries in . . . and FATHER disappears into darkness . . . coughing, the black cloth trailing behind him.

Get off the roof, you got no respect, you stupid?

Underground sound stops. NURSE, carrying a bowl of water and cloth, heads straight for the cast. She takes his hand, patting it as he whimpers.

NURSE. All right now, let's come back, come on, dear, come on back . . . (*He stops struggling and opens his eyes.*)

LYMAN. Wah. Oh. What dreams. God, how I'd like to be dead.

NURSE. Don't start feeling sorry for yourself; you know what they say – come down off the cross, they need the wood.

LYMAN. I'm suffocating, can't you open a window?

NURSE. Not any more, I can't.

LYMAN. Huh? – Oh, listen, that's ridiculous, I wasn't trying to climb out, it was just those pills got me crazy . . .

NURSE. Well, maybe later. I got to wash up now. Your lawyer's asking can he come in . . .

LYMAN. I thought he'd gone back to New York. I look terrible?

NURSE (*she swabs his face and hands*). You takin' it too hard. Be different if you deserted those women, but anybody can see how well taken care of they are . . .

LYMAN. Go on, you don't kid me, Hogan – underneath all this cool you know you're shocked as hell.

NURSE. Go on, brush your teeth. (*As he does.*) The last shock I had come off a short in my vacuum cleaner . . . (*He laughs, then groans in pain.*) One thing I *have* been wondering, though.

LYMAN. What've you been wondering?

NURSE. Whatever got into you to actually marry that woman? – Man as smart as you?

LYMAN. Were you talking about ice before?

NURSE. Ice? Oh, you mean . . . ya, we go ice fishing on the lake, me and my husband and my boy. – You're remembering a lot better now.

LYMAN (*staring*). It's going to seem very peculiar – I've never not been married, you know. I have a feeling it's like suddenly your case has been dismissed and you don't have to be in court any more.

NURSE. Don't you talk bad about those women; they don't look mean to me.

LYMAN. I just never felt such jealousy, for one thing, and I've known a lot of women. And she had a fantastic smell; Leah smelled like a ripe, pink, slightly musty cantaloupe. And her smile – when she showed her teeth her clothes seemed to drop off. I don't know, we had some prehistoric kind of connection – I swear, if I was blindfolded and a dozen women walked past me on a sidewalk I could pick out the clack of her heels. I even loved lying in bed listening to the quiet splash of her bath water. And of course slipping into her soft cathedral . . .

NURSE. You have the dirtiest mind I ever seen on an educated man.

LYMAN. I couldn't lose her, Hogan. I couldn't lose her. I could not lose her, and that's why I married her. And those are all good reasons, unless you're married already.

NURSE. I'll get your lawyer, okay?

He seems suddenly overcome, weeps.

Now don't you start that cryin' again . . .

LYMAN. It's just my children . . . you can't imagine how they respected me . . . that's the one thing I just can't deal with . . . (*Bracing himself.*) But nobody's any better, goddamit!

TOM WILSON *enters.*

TOM. May I come in?

LYMAN (*uncertainty, trying to read* TOM). Hi! I thought you'd gone back – something happen?

TOM. Can we talk?

NURSE *exits*.

LYMAN. If you can bear it. (*Grins.*) You despise me, Tom?

TOM. I'm still staggering, I don't know what I think.

LYMAN. Sure you do, but that's okay. (*His charming grin.*) What's up?

TOM. I've been discussing things with the women . . .

LYMAN. I can't bear talking about them – I thought I told you – or did I? – just give them what they want. Within reason, I mean.

TOM. That's the thing – I'm not sure they know what they want.

LYMAN. Go on – they want to kill me, don't they?

TOM. Oh, no doubt about *that*, but . . . I really believe Theo'd like to find a way to forgive you.

LYMAN. Oh no! – that's impossible!

TOM. She's a great spirit, Lyman.

LYMAN. . . . Not that great; I'd have to live on my knees the rest of my life.

TOM. Maybe not – if you were clear about yourselves and came to an understanding . . .

LYMAN. I'm pretty clear now – I'm a selfish son of a bitch. But I have loved the truth.

TOM. And what's the truth?

LYMAN. A man can be faithful to himself or to other people – but not to both. At least not happily. We all know this, but it's immoral to admit it – the first law of life is betrayal; why else did those Rabbis pick Cain and Abel to open the Bible?

TOM. But the Bible doesn't end there, does it?

LYMAN. Jesus Christ? I can't worship self-denial; excuse me, but it's just not true for me. We're all ego, kid, ego plus an occasional prayer.

TOM. Then why'd you bother building one of the most socially responsible companies in America?

LYMAN. The truth? I did that twenty-five years ago, when

I was still trying to deny my unrighteousness. But I don't deny anything any more. – What should I say to them, Tom? What should I do?

TOM. Am I wrong? – You seem deeply depressed.

LYMAN. I dread seeing them again. Especially Bessie. I absolutely can't bear the thought of her . . . Advise me, tell me something.

TOM. Maybe you ought to give up trying to seem so strong.

Slight pause.

LYMAN. What do you want me to say, I'm a loser?

TOM. Well? Right now – aren't you?

LYMAN. Well . . . no, goddamit. A loser has lived somebody else's life, I've lived my own; crappy as it may seem, it's mine. And I'm no worse than anybody else! – Now answer that, and don't kid me.

TOM. All right, I won't kid you; I think you've done these women terrible harm.

LYMAN. You do.

TOM. Theo especially. I think you've raked her soul. If you want to get off this dime you're on I'd begin by confronting that.

LYMAN. I've also given her an interesting life, a terrific daughter, and made her very rich. I mean, exactly what harm are you talking about?

TOM. Lyman, you deceived her . . .

LYMAN (*fury overtaking him*). But she couldn't have had all that if I hadn't deceived her! – you know as well as I that nobody could live with Theo for more than a month without some relief! I've suffered at least as much as she has in this fucking marriage!

TOM (*demurring*). Well . . .

LYMAN. . . . Now listen, you want the rock bottom truth? – I curse the day I ever laid eyes on her and I don't *want* her forgiveness!

TOM. For Pete's sake don't get angry . . .

LYMAN (*instantly caught in his memory*). But your whole picture is just untrue! I ever tell you how we met? – Let's stop talking as though this marriage was made in heaven, for Christ's sake! – I was hitchhiking back from Cornell; nineteen innocent years of age; I'm standing beside the road with my suitcase, and I have to take a leak. So I leave the suitcase and go behind a bush. This minister sees the suitcase and stops, gives me a ride and I end up at an Audubon Society picnic where, lo and behold, I meet his daughter, Theodora. – Had I taken that suitcase with me behind the bush I'd never have met her! – And serious people still go around looking for the moral purpose of the universe.

TOM. Give or take a bad patch or two, you've had the best marriage of anyone I ever met.

LYMAN (*a sigh*). I know. – Look, we're all the same; a man is a fourteen-room house – in the bedroom he's asleep with his intelligent wife, in the living room he's rolling around with some bareass girl, in the library he's paying his taxes, in the yard he's raising tomatoes, and in the cellar he's making a bomb to blow it all up. And nobody's different . . . Except you, maybe. Are you?

TOM. I don't raise tomatoes . . . Listen, the TV is flogging the story and it's humiliating for the women; let's settle on a statement and be done with it. What do you want?

LYMAN. What I always wanted; both of them.

TOM. Be serious . . .

LYMAN. I know those women, and they still love me! It's only what they think they're *supposed* to feel that's confusing them. – Do I sound crazy?

TOM. There's something else we have to discuss . . .

LYMAN. – What's Leah saying . . . anything?

TOM. She's stunned. But frankly, I'm not sure she's out of the question either . . . if that's the move you wanted to make.

LYMAN (*deeply touched*). What size these women have! I wish I was struck dead! (*Weeping threatens again.*) Oh, Tom, I'm lost!

TOM. . . . I'm sorry, but there's one urgent thing. I got a call from Jeff Huddleston at six this morning. He heard it on the radio. He's going to insist you resign from the board.

LYMAN. Not on your life! – I started that company and I'm keeping it! – It's outrageous! – Jeff Huddleston's got a woman stashed in Trump Tower and two in L.A.

TOM. *Huddleston?*

LYMAN. – He offered to loan me one once! Huddleston has more outside ass than a Nevada whorehouse!

TOM. But he doesn't marry them.

LYMAN. Right! – In other words, what I really violated was the law of hypocrisy.

TOM. Unfortunately, that's the one that operates.

LYMAN. Yes. Well not with me, kid – what I wish I do!

BESSIE and THEO enter. THEO stands beside his bed staring at him without expression. BESSIE doesn't so much as look directly at him. After a long moment . . .

LYMAN (*downing fear*). My God, Theo – thank you . . . I mean for coming. I didn't expect you . . .

She sits down in a potent silence. BESSIE remains standing, fiercely aloof. He is openly and awkwardly ashamed . . .

. . . Hi, Bessie.

BESSIE. I'm here for her sake, she wanted to say something to you. (*Hurrying her along.*) Mother?

But THEO takes no notice, staring at LYMAN with a fixed, unreadable smile. After a long awkward moment . . .

LYMAN (*to fill the void*). How are you feeling today? I heard you were . . .

THEO (*dead flat; it cuts him off*). I won't be seeing you again, Lyman.

LYMAN. Yes, well . . . I guess there's no use apologizing, you know my character . . . I am sorry, though.

THEO. I can't leave my life lying all over the floor like this.

LYMAN. I'll talk about anything you like, Theo. Make it as tough as you want to.

THEO. I seem confused but I'm not; there's just so much that I . . . that I don't want bottled up in me any more.

LYMAN. Sure, I understand.

THEO. – Do you remember that young English instructor whose wife had walked out on him – and his advice to you about sex?

LYMAN. An English instructor?

THEO. 'Bend it in half,' he said, 'and tie a rubber band around it.'

LYMAN (*laughs, but a little alarmed*). Oh, sure, Jim Donaldson!

THEO. Everyone used to laugh at that.

LYMAN (*her smile is empty, his charm desperate*). Right! 'Bend it in half and . . .' (*Continues a strained chuckling.*)

THEO (*cutting him off*). I *hated* you laughing at that; it showed a vulgar and disgusting side of you. I was ashamed . . . for you and for myself.

LYMAN (*brought up short*). I see. But that's so long ago, Theo . . .

THEO. I nearly ended it right then and there, but I thought I was too inexperienced to make a judgement on something like that. But I was right – you *were* a vulgar, unfeeling man, and you are still.

Anxiously, he glances over to BESSIE *for help or explanation of this weirdness.*

LYMAN. I see. Well, I guess our whole life was a mistake then. (*Angered but attempting charm.*) But I made a good living.

BESSIE. Please, Mother, let's go, he's mocking you, can't you hear it?

LYMAN (*flaring up*). Must I not defend myself? Am I supposed to lie and be destroyed? – Please go ahead, Theo, I'm listening, I understand what you're saying, and it's okay, it's what you feel.

THEO (*seeming perfectly relaxed*). – What was the name of the river, about half an hour's walk past the Chemistry Building?

LYMAN (*puzzled . . . is she mad?*). What river?

THEO. Where we went skinny dipping with those geologists and their girls . . .

LYMAN (*at a loss for a moment, then . . .*). Oh, you mean graduation night. . . !

THEO. . . . The whole crowd swimming naked at the falls . . . and their girls all laughing in the darkness. . . ?

LYMAN (*starting to smile – uncomprehending*). Oh, sure . . . that was a great night!

THEO. I straddled you, and over your shoulder . . . did I dream this? – I recall a white wall of limestone, rising straight out of the river. . . ?

LYMAN. That's right, Devonian. It was full of fossils.

THEO. Yes! Beetle imprints, worm tracks, crustacea fifty million years old going straight up like a white temple wall . . . and we floating around below, like two frogs attached in the darkness . . . our wet eyelashes touching.

LYMAN. Yes.

THEO. It was very beautiful, that evening.

LYMAN. I'm glad you remember it that way.

THEO. You see, I am not at all a Puritan, it is simply a question of taste – that night was inspiring.

LYMAN. Well, I never had taste, we both know that. But I'm not going to lie to you, Theo – taste to me is what's left of life after people can't screw any more.

THEO. You should have told me that thirty years ago.

LYMAN. I didn't know it thirty years ago.

THEO. And do you remember what you said as we floated there?

LYMAN (*hesitates*). Yes.

THEO. No you don't.

LYMAN. I said, 'What could ever come between us?'.

THEO (*immense wonder and relief*). Yes. And did you mean that then? Or was I naive to believe you? Please tell me the truth.

LYMAN (*affected*). Yes, I believed it.

THEO. When did you begin to fool me?

LYMAN. Please don't go on any more . . .

THEO. I am trying to pinpoint when my life died. Just so I can know; that's not unreasonable, is it?

LYMAN. From my heart, Theo – I ask your pardon.

THEO. – When did Billie Holliday die?

LYMAN. Billie Holliday? – oh, I don't know, ten – twelve years ago? Why?

She goes silent, stares into space. He is suddenly on the verge of weeping at the sight of her suffering.

Oh, Theo, I'm so sorry . . . (*She remains staring.*) Why do you want to know about Billie . . . ?

BESSIE. All right, Mother, let's go, huh?

LYMAN. Bessie, I think it might be better if she talked it out . . .

BESSIE. No one is interested in what you think. (*To* THEO.) I want you to come now!

LYMAN. Have mercy on her!

BESSIE. *You* talking mercy!?

LYMAN. For her, not me! – She loved me! Don't you hear what she's trying to say?

BESSIE. How can you listen to this shit!

LYMAN. How dare you! I gave you a damned fine life, Bessie!

BESSIE. You have nothing to say any more, you are a nonsense!

THEO. Please, dear! – Wait outside for a few minutes.

BESSIE, *seeing her adamant, strides out.*

You've torn out her heart.

He turns away trying not to weep.

Was there some pleasure in making a fool of me? What was behind this? Why couldn't you have told me about this woman?

LYMAN. I did try, many times, but . . . I guess it sounds crazy, but . . . I just couldn't bear to lose you.

THEO. But – ! (*Sudden, near-hysterical intensity.*) – You were

lying to me every day all these nine or ten years, and before
that about other women, weren't you? – what would you
possibly lose?

LYMAN (*determined not to flinch*). . . . Your happiness.

THEO. *My* happiness!

LYMAN. I love you.

THEO. You love me.

LYMAN. (*daring to, after a hesitation*). Only the truth can
help us, Theo – I think you were happier in these last years
than ever in our marriage – you feel that, don't you?

She doesn't contradict.

And I think the reason is that I was never bored being
with you.

THEO. You'd been bored with me?

LYMAN. Same as you'd been with me, dear . . . I'm talking
about – you know – just normal marital boredom.

But she seems obtuse to this, so he tries to explain.

You know, like at dinner – when I'd repeat some story
you'd heard a thousand times . . . ? Like my grandfather
losing three fingers under the Ninth Avenue trolley . . . ?

THEO. But I loved that story! I was *never* bored with you
. . . stupid as that was.

LYMAN (*now she just seems perverse*). Theo, you were bored
– it's no sin! Same as I was when you'd start telling
people for the ten thousandth time that – for instance
. . . (*His charming laugh.*) as a minister's daughter you
were not permitted to climb a tree and show off your
panties?

THEO (*sternly resisting his charm*). But I think people are
interested in a kind of society that has completely
disappeared! That story has historical importance!

LYMAN (*the full agony*). But darling, that story is engraved
in my flesh! . . . And I beg you, don't make this a moral
dilemma, it's simply a question of reading the same page
of a newspaper for thirty years! It is just common ordinary
domestic tedium, dear, it is life, and there's no other

woman I know who has the honesty and strength to accept it as life – if you wanted to!

THEO (*a pause; above her confusion, she is striving desperately to understand*). And why do you say I was happier in these last years?

LYMAN. Because you could see my contentment, and I was content . . .

THEO. Because she . . . ?

LYMAN. Because whenever you started with your panties again I could still find you lovable, knowing that the story was not going to be my entire fate till the day I died.

THEO. . . . Because she was waiting for you.

LYMAN. Right.

THEO. You were never bored with *her*?

LYMAN. Oh God yes! Sometimes even more than with you.

THEO (*quick intense hopeful curiosity*). Really! And what then?

LYMAN. Then I would thank my luck that I had you to come back to. – I know how hard this is to understand, Theo.

THEO. No-no . . . I guess I've always known it.

LYMAN. What?

THEO. You are some kind of . . . of giant clam.

LYMAN. Clam?

THEO. Waiting on the bottom for whatever happens to fall from the ocean into your mouth; you are simply a craving, and that craving you call love. You are a kind of monster, and I think you even know it, don't you? I can almost begin to pity you, Lyman. (*She turns to leave.*) I hope you make a good recovery. It's all very clear now, I'm glad I stayed.

LYMAN. It's amazing – the minute the mystery of life appears, you think everything's cleared up.

THEO. There's no mystery to me, you have never loved anyone!

LYMAN. Then explain to yourself how this worthless, loveless, treacherous clam, could have single-handedly made two such different women happier than they'd ever been in their lives!

THEO. Really! (*Laughs ending in a near-scream.*) Really and truly *happy*?!

LYMAN (*stepping out of the cast, outraged –* THEO *remaining fixed on the cast*). . . . In fact, if I dared admit the whole idiotic truth, the only one who suffered these past nine years – was *me*!

An enormous echoing roar fills the theatre – the roar of a lion.

Light rises on BESSIE *looking front through field glasses; she is wearing shorts and pith helmet and khaki safari jacket.*

THEO. *You suffering?* – oh dear God save us!

She is trying to sustain her bitter laughing and moves toward BESSIE, *and as she enters the area her laughter dies off and she takes a pith helmet out of a picnic basket and puts it on.*

LYMAN *follows* THEO. *There is no dialogue break.*

LYMAN. . . . What would you call it, then – having to look into your innocent, contented faces, when I knew the hollowness your happiness was based on? That isn't suffering?

He takes his place beside the two women, looking in the same direction out front, shading his eyes. With no break in dialogue . . .

BESSIE (*looking through field glasses*). Good heavens, is he going to mount her *again*?

LYMAN. They don't call him King of the Beasts for nothing, honey.

BESSIE. Poor thing, how patient she is.

THEO (*taking the glasses from her*). Oh come, dear, she's not *only* patient.

BESSIE (*spreading a table cloth on the ground and picnic things*). But it's only once every half a year, isn't it?

LYMAN. Once that we *know* about.

THEO (*helping spread the picnic*). Oh no, they're marvellously loyal couples.

LYMAN. No, dear, they have harems; you're thinking of storks.

BESSIE (*offering an egg*). Daddy?

LYMAN (*sitting – happily eating*). I love you in those helmets, you look like two noble ladies on safari.

THEO (*stretching out on the ground*). The air here! The silence. These hills.

BESSIE. Thanks for bringing me, Daddy. I'm so sorry Harold had to do those lectures. I'll never forget this trip. – Why do you look sad?

LYMAN. Me? No.

THEO. It's just guilt.

LYMAN (*alarmed*). Guilt?

THEO. He's been away from the office for a whole week.

LYMAN (*relieved*). Oh. Actually, why do we think of monogamy as a higher form of life?

THEO. Well, it implies an intensification of love.

LYMAN. How about that, Bess? You had a lot of boyfriends before Harold, didn't you?

BESSIE. Well . . . yes, I guess it is more intense with one.

LYMAN. But how does that make it a higher form?

THEO. Monogamy strengthens the family; random screwing undermines it.

LYMAN. But as one neurotic to another, what's so good about strengthening the family?

THEO. Well, for one thing it enhances liberty.

BESSIE (*puzzled*). Liberty? Really?

THEO. The family disciplines its members; when the family is weak the state has to move in; so the stronger the family the fewer the police. And that is why monogamy is a higher form.

LYMAN. Jesus, did you just make that up? (*To* BESSIE.) Isn't she marvellous? I'm giving her an A-plus!

THEO (*happily hurt*). Oh shut up.

LYMAN. But what about the Muslims? They're very big

on stable families but a lot of them have two or three
wives.

THEO. But only one is really the *wife*.

LYMAN. Not according to my father – they often had two
main women, one to run the house and one for the bed.
But they were both serious wives.

THEO. Your father's sociology was on a par with his morals
– non-existent.

LYMAN (*laughs; to* BESSIE). Your mother is a classical
woman, you know why?

BESSIE (*laughing delightedly*). Why?

LYMAN. Because she is always clear and consistent and . . .

THEO. . . . Rather boring.

*He guffaws warmly, clapping his hands over his head in
appreciation.*

BESSIE. You are not boring! (*Rushing to embrace* THEO.)
Tell her she is not boring!

LYMAN (*embracing* THEO *with* BESSIE). Please no . . . I
swear I didn't mean boring!

THEO (*tearfully hurt*). Well I'd rather be boring and clear
than cute and stupid!

BESSIE. But I don't think he meant . . .

LYMAN. Who asked you to be cute?

THEO (*a tortured look*). I wish I knew how to amuse you!

LYMAN. I swear to God I am not bored, Theo! – Now
please don't go on about it!

THEO. Your eyes have been glazed over since we stepped
onto this wretched continent!

LYMAN (*guiltily stretching an awkward embrace toward her*).
I *love* this trip, and being with both of you. . . ! Theo,
please! – Now you are making me guilty!

The lion's roar interrupts and they all look front in shock.

BESSIE. Is he heading here. . . ? Daddy! – He's trotting!

GUIDE'S VOICE (*off on bullhorn*). You will have to come
back to the car, everyone! At once!

LYMAN. Quick!

He pushes both women off.

BESSIE (*on exiting*). Daddy, come. . . !
THEO (*sensing he is remaining behind*). Lyman. . . ?
LYMAN. Go!

He pushes her off, but turns back himself.

GUIDE'S VOICE. Come back to the car at once, Mr Felt!

Lion's roar – but closer now. LYMAN *facing front and the lion, prepared to run for it but holding his ground.*

Mr Felt, get back to the car!

Another roar!

LYMAN (*eyes on the 'lion', shouting toward it with fear's exhilaration*). I *am* happy, yes! That I'm married to Theodora and have Bessie . . . yes, *and Leah, too*!

Another roar!

BESSIE (*from a distance*). Daddy, please come here!
LYMAN. And that I've made a mountain of money . . . yes, and have no pending lawsuits! –
BESSIE (*from a distance*). Daddy. . . !
LYMAN (*flinging his words toward the approaching beast, but crouched and ready to flee*). . . . And that I don't sacrifice one precious day to things I don't believe in – and that includes monogamy, yes, we love our lives, you goddam lion!

Wide-eyed, still crouched to run, he is watching the approaching lion – whose roar, as we now hear, has changed to a rather more relaxed guttural growling, much diminished; and LYMAN *cautiously straightens up, and turns triumphantly toward the women offstage. And* BESSIE *flies out and throws her arms around him in ecstatic relief, kissing him.*

BESSIE (*looking front*). Daddy, he turned back! What did you do that for!

THEO *enters.*

THEO. He turned back! (*To him.*) How did you do that! (*To* BESSIE.) Did you see how he stopped and looked at him and turned around? (*To* LYMAN.) What happened?

LYMAN. I think . . . he sensed that I – darling, I think I've lost my guilt!

THEO. What!

LYMAN (*staring in wonder*). His roar hit my teeth like voltage and suddenly, it was so clear that . . . (*Turns to her.*) I've always been happy with you, Theo! – I'm a happy man and I am never going to apologize for it again!

THEO (*tears of gratitude, clasping her hands together prayerfully*). Oh, Lyman! (*Rushing to kiss him.*) Oh, darling!

LYMAN (*still riding his wave, holding out his hand to her*). What old good friends we are, Theo! Put her there! (*She laughs and manfully shakes hands.*) What a *person* you are, what a grave and beautiful face you have!

BESSIE. Oh, Daddy, that's so lovely! – You're just *marvellous*! (*She weeps.*)

LYMAN. How the hell are we still together – do you realize how she must love me to stand for my character? Well I love her too! I definitely worship this woman, Bessie!

THEO. Oh, this is what I always saw happening some day! (*A sophisticated laugh.*) – Not with a lion, of course, but exactly this sudden flash of light. . . !

LYMAN. The whole future is clear to me now! We are not going to sidle shamefully into our late middle age, we're marching in heads up! I'm going to build a selfish little cottage in the Caribbean and we'll fill it up with all the thick English novels we never got to finish . . . plus Proust! – and I'll buy two mopeds with little baskets on the handlebars for the shopping trips . . .

THEO. I knew it, I knew it!

LYMAN. . . . And I'll spend every day with you – except maybe a week or two a month in the Elmira office!

BESSIE. How fantastic, Mother!

THEO. Thank you, lion! Thank you, Africa! (*Turning to him.*) Lyman?

LYMAN (*already mentally departing the present*). . . . Huh?

Yes!

THEO. I am all new!

She throws her arms around him, burying her face in his neck. He looks front with an expression of deepening agony.

BESSIE. This has been the most fantastic two weeks of my life! I love you, Daddy!

She rushes to him and with one arm he embraces her, the other around THEO; *tears starting into his eyes.*

BESSIE. Are you weeping?

LYMAN. Just amazement, honey . . . at my luck, I guess. Come, we'd better go back.

Sombrely he turns them upstage; lights are changing, growing dimmer and they walk into darkness while he remains behind. Alone – in his hospital gown still – he slowly turns front; light spreads and reveals the NURSE *sitting near the bed and cast.*

NURSE (*to the cast, exactly as earlier*). The only thing I don't understand is why you married that woman, a smart man like you.

LYMAN *stares ahead as* LEAH *appears, isolated in light; she is in her fur coat, exactly as in Act One when she was about to go for an abortion. The* NURSE *remains on the periphery, immobile.*

LEAH. Yes, I suppose it could wait a week or so, but . . . really, Lyman, you know you're never going to leave her.

LYMAN. You cancel the operation, okay? And I'm telling her tomorrow.

LEAH. You're telling her what?

LYMAN (*almost holding his breath*). I will not rationalize you away. I have one life! I'm going to ask her for a divorce.

LEAH. My God, Lyman!

LYMAN (*pulls her into his arms*). Why are we so *connected*? – Do you feel it?

LEAH. I don't understand it. I seem to have known you forever. But listen, I know your attachment to her . . .

LYMAN. I trust you . . . I'd like to tell you something. (*He takes a pause out of sheer caution.*) I had a son once, with a terrific girl I knew. A long time ago now. – I'm ashamed of this – I convinced her to have it. I was crazy about her. But I had to break it off or lose my marriage. It was torture. – About seventeen years later I am checking into Pan Am in Los Angeles, and I see this young guy in line in front of me. My spitting image. Unmistakable. When he laid his ticket on the counter the clerk said his name, sure enough – it was his mother's. We sat facing each other in the waiting area. I was paralyzed.

LEAH. Why couldn't you have introduced yourself!

LYMAN. Well, he was dressed kind of poor . . . and he had an unhappy look. He'd have to feel I'd betrayed him, I was sure he'd hate me . . . (*Pause; he kisses her hand.*) Please keep this baby. Will you? And stay home and cross your legs, you hear? – no dates.

LEAH. But stop worrying about another man, okay? – Please, I'm not really like that, if I'm committed.

LYMAN (*with mock anger squeezes her cheeks together*). A nunnery for you till I get back, you hear?

LEAH. This is serious?

LYMAN. This is serious.

LEAH. Suddenly . . . why am I not sure I want to be a mother! – Do I, you think?

LYMAN. Yes you do, I think!

Kisses her. They laugh together. He turns to leave; she grasps his hands and presses them together between hers in a prayerful gesture; and facing heaven . . .

LEAH. Please! Some good luck! (*To him directly.*) Why is everything so dangerous!

She gives him a violent kiss. She walks into darkness and, as he turns, THEO *appears walking; she is hiding something behind her back and smiling lovingly.* LYMAN *looks solemn, prepared for the showdown.*

LYMAN. Theo, dear . . . There's something I have to tell you . . .

THEO (*holding out a cashmere sweater*). Happy birthday!

LYMAN (*startled*). Hah? But it's not July, is it!

THEO. But it was so sinfully expensive I needed an excuse. (*Putting him into the sweater.*) Here . . . straighten it. It's Italian. It's not too big, is it? (*Stepping back to admire.*) It's gorgeous, look in the mirror!

LYMAN. It's beautiful, thank you, dear. But listen, I really have something to . . .

THEO. My God, Lyman, you are simply magnificent! (*Linking arms and walking in her cumbersome way.*) I have another surprise – I got tickets for the Ballanchine! And a table at Luigi's afterwards!

LYMAN (*grimly screwing up his courage – and he is beginning to resent her domination*). I have something to tell you, Theo, why do you make it so hard for me!

THEO. What?

He is paralyzed.

What is it? Has something happened? (*Alarmed now.*) Lyman! (*Asking.*) – You went for your checkup!

LYMAN (*about to explode*). God's sake, no, it's not that!

THEO. Why is your face so grey? Please, what is it, you look terrified!

He moves away from her and her awful caring, and halts facing front. She moves off and calls to him from the distance.

– I'll ring my cousin Wilbur, he's still at Mass. General, we can go up there together. . . ! Please, darling, don't worry about anything. . . ! What is it, can you tell me?

In total blockage – both in the past and present – he inhales deeply and lets out a gigantic long howl, arms raised, imploring heaven for relief. In effect, it blasts her out of his mind – she de-animates and goes dark, and he is alone again.

LYMAN (*to himself, facing front*). No guts. That's the whole story. No guts!

A hospital gurney rolls on. LEAH *is lying on it. She raises up on her elbows.*

LEAH. You got here!

LYMAN (*grinning broadly*). Of course I got here!

LEAH. Have they shown him to you? He's a boy! – And you see how he looks like you?

LYMAN. No, not me – like my father after a shave. (*Kisses her.*) What an airy softness on your eyes; like God leaned down and lightly kissed your breast.

LEAH. I was so hoping you'd come. (*Kisses his hand.*) Thank you for him, darling. I love you. And I do understand why you can't divorce her, and it's okay. Really. In fact, it's ironical, you make me understand what real commitment means.

LYMAN. I love you, Leah. You have a sublime gift of nearness . . .

LEAH. You'll still come and see us, won't you? – When you can? (*He covers his face.*) Don't feel bad, we could still have a good life! What can I name him?

LYMAN (*lowering his hands, in the throes of loss*). I filled out the form for you.

LEAH (*laughs*). You did?

LYMAN. I put down Benjamin, is that okay?

LEAH. If it's from you it's beautiful. What about a second name? – I guess mine, huh?

LYMAN. I want to put down Felt. – In fact, I did.

LEAH. Felt! – How will I explain that to him?

LYMAN (*hesitates . . . then, with a tense smile . . .*) I know you owe me nothing, darling, but they tell me there's been a man coming in to see you.

LEAH. A doctor; he stops by; I used to know him. But truthfully . . . I do feel more sure I'm going to end up married. Maybe not, but definitely maybe – I mean some day.

LYMAN. With who?

LEAH. I don't know! When I came out of the anaesthetic, I thought – maybe if I was married we could both be guilty, and it would make it easier for you.

LYMAN. I'm not even going to try to understand that.

LEAH (*laughing, she suddenly weeps* . . .). Please go, dear, I can't bear this . . . Come later if you can or just write me – or call me up and make me laugh!

LYMAN. Oh, my darling, my darling . . . we've got to stay together!

LEAH (*angering*). But you can't! – Why do you keep saying that!

LYMAN. What if I got you a loft downtown in the city, and I'd buy you out here and you can stay home with him and paint? – What do you say? I'd set up a trust fund . . .

LEAH. Why don't we just play it by ear?

LYMAN. Meaning what?

LEAH. Come up when you can, and we'll meet in the city sometimes when I come down . . .

LYMAN. . . . My heart's going to die . . . you're drifting away!

LEAH (*direct and tough*). . . . But how can I commit myself and you just stop by now and then. . . . I mean sooner or later won't that irritate me? – You poor man, you're so divided . . . or do you think you're too old?

Tremendously conflicted, he avoids her eyes. She strokes his face.

Well, don't get depressed; we are how we are. . . . Anyway, I'm not absolutely sure I should be married to anybody – I think I may still be too curious.

LYMAN. About men?

She nods, mystified. He is suddenly decisive.

Give me a month. By June first I either settle with Theo or I disappear, okay?

LEAH. You poor man. I wish I could help you, but I'm so mixed up myself . . .

LYMAN. I've lost my judgement, I'm out of sync with my age and I'm being foolish.

LEAH. But you are not old, you're a sensualist and romantic, and I think it's just marvellous!

LYMAN (*he is moving into a light and she is vanishing*). No! I know what's wrong with me – I could never stand still for death! Which you've got to do, by a certain age, or be ridiculous – you've got to stand there nobly and serene . . .

LEAH *is gone now, he's alone.*

. . . and let death run his tape out your arms and around your belly and up your crotch until he's got you fitted for that last black suit. And I can't, I won't! . . . So I'm left wrestling with this anachronistic energy which . . .

as he enters the cast, crying out to the world . . .

. . . God has charged me with and I will use it till the dirt is shovelled into my mouth! Life! Life! Fuck death and dying!

Light widens, finding LEAH *in the present, dressed differently than in the previous – in her fur coat – standing near the bed with the* NURSE, *listening to his shouts.*

NURSE. Don't be afraid, just wait a minute, he comes out of it. I'm sure he wants to see you.

LEAH (*moving tentatively to the cast*). Lyman?

He looks at her with cloudy recognition.

It's me, Leah.

NURSE *exits.*

LYMAN (*now fully aware of her*). Leah! (*Turning away from her.*) Jesus, what have I done to you! – Wait . . . (*A moment; he looks around.*) Was Theo here?

LEAH. I think she's gone, I just got here.

LYMAN. I don't know where the hell I am. . . . Oh, Leah, it's sitting on my chest like a bag of cement.

LEAH. What is?

LYMAN. My character.

LEAH. Yes, well . . . it's pretty bad.

LYMAN. And still, I swear, all I've ever done is try to be honest. (*Moved.*) Thanks for coming.

LEAH. I only came about Benny, I don't know how to begin explaining this to him.

LYMAN (*about to weep again*). What balls you have to come here and talk so coolly, I really salute you. – What's he saying?

LEAH (*frustrated, she turns away*). He's excited that he has a sister.

LYMAN (*painful admiration*). Oh, that dear boy!

LEAH. He's very badly mixed up, Lyman; he's seen us all on TV and one of the other kids told him he has two mothers. He sweats in his sleep. He keeps asking me are you coming home again. It's twisting my heart. I'm terrified if this isn't settled right it could screw up the rest of his life. (*Tears start.*) You're his idol, Lyman! – His god!

LYMAN. Oh, the wreckage, the wreckage . . .

LEAH. Tell me the truth; it's okay if you don't, I just want to know – do you feel a responsibility or not?

LYMAN (*flaring up, scared as much as indignant*). How can you ask such a thing?

LEAH. Why! That's a reasonable question!

LYMAN. Now you listen – I know I'm wrong and I'm wrong and I'm wrong but I did not throw you both across my saddle to rape you in my tent! You knew I was married, and you tried to make me love you, so I'm not entirely . . .

LEAH. Lyman, if you're blaming me I'm going to sink through this floor!

LYMAN. I'm talking about truth not blame – this is not entirely a one-man disaster!

LEAH. It's amazing, the minute you talk about truth you always come out looking better than anybody else!

LYMAN. Now that's unfair!

LEAH (*slight pause*). I want to talk about Benny.

LYMAN. You could bring him tomorrow if you like. But go ahead, we can talk now.

A pause as she settles down.

LEAH (*a flushed grin*). Incidentally . . . I'm just curious, how's everything with your wife? – They tell me you spent over an hour with her.

LYMAN. All she did was sit there telling me I'm a monster who never loved anybody.

LEAH (*with a hard grin*). And I suppose you reassured her otherwise.

LYMAN. Well, I did love her. Just as I loved you. The truth is the truth, kid.

LEAH. What a piece of work you are, Lyman, really – you go falling off a mountain and you still don't understand anything.

LYMAN. What should I understand?

LEAH. Never mind.

LYMAN. Well what?

LEAH (*anxiety and anger*). It's no business of mine, but your hatred for that woman is monumental. I mean it's . . . *oceanic*.

LYMAN. What the hell are you going on about!

LEAH. Because it's unnerving to have to listen to this shit all over again!

LYMAN. What shit? What have I said!

LEAH. My dear man, in case it slipped your mind, when I was two months pregnant we went to New York and you picked the Carlyle Hotel to stay at – four blocks from your house! 'Loved her' – good G. . . !

A window begins to appear upstage with THEO *seated in profile, reading a book. He is staring as he emerges from the cast, turning to look up at the window . . .* LEAH *goes on with no pause.*

What was all that about if it wasn't hatred! – And walking
me past your front window with her sitting there. . . ?
And – yes, my God I almost forgot – going in to see her
yet? You had murder in you and you still do! – probably
for me too!

LYMAN (*glancing up at* THEO *in the window*). But it didn't
feel like murder at all. I was dancing the high wire on
the edge of the world . . . finally risking everything to
find myself! – Strolling with you past my house, the
spring breeze, the lingerie in the Madison Avenue shop
windows, the swish of . . . wasn't it a taffeta skirt you
wore? . . . and my new baby coiled in your belly? – I'd
beaten guilt forever!

She is moving toward him, part of his recall.

. . . And how languorous you were, your pregnant glory
bulging under the streetlamp!

She takes on the ease of that long-ago stroll, and. . . .

LEAH. Is that her?

LYMAN *looks up at* THEO *then at* LEAH, *inspired, alive.*

LYMAN. Oh, Leah darling, how sexy you look against tall
buildings.

LEAH (*warm smile, taking his arm*). You're tense, aren't
you?

LYMAN. Well, I've lived here with her for so many years . . .

LEAH. Was she very upset when you told her?

LYMAN (*tragically; but hesitates*). . . . Yes, dear, she was.

LEAH. Well, maybe she'll marry again in time.

LYMAN (*a glance to the window; he loosens her grip on his
arm*). I doubt it, somehow.

LEAH (*an intrigued smile*). Mustn't we touch?

LYMAN (*quickly regaining her arm*). Of course!

They start walking away.

LEAH. I'd love to meet her some time . . . just as friends.

LYMAN. You might.

LEAH. You're still feeling guilty, aren't you?

LYMAN (*halts; a strange determination suddenly*). A little, yes. And I hate it. – Listen, I'd like to see if I can go in and say hello.

LEAH. Really? Would you like me to come?

LYMAN. Not just yet. Would you mind a lot? Tell me.

LEAH. No, go ahead. I kind of like it that you don't just drop people.

LYMAN. God, you have balls! I'll see you back at the hotel in twenty minutes, okay?

LEAH. Take your time! I'll play with all that gorgeous underwear you bought. (*Touching her belly.*) I'm so contented, Lyman!

She turns and walks away. He remains below the window, staring at her departing figure.

LYMAN. Why is it, the happier she is the sadder I get? It's this damned *objectivity*! – Like God must feel when he looks at happy people – knowing what he knows about worms! (*Now he looks up at* THEO, *and his heart sinks.*) What have I done! Have I only doubled the distance that I stand from my life? (*Violent determination.*) Idiot! – love her! Now that she doesn't deprive you any more let love flow to your wise and wonderful wife! To hell with this guilt!

He rushes toward THEO, *but then turns away in terror, walking around in a circle and blowing out air and covering his face. Now gritting his teeth he again hurries toward the window . . . which disappears, as she rises, startled.*

THEO. Lyman! – you said Tuesday, didn't you?

He takes her in his arms, kisses her with frantic passion. She is surprised and happy.

LYMAN. What a handsome lady! Theo, you are God's handwriting.

LEAH. Ralph Waldo Emerson.

LYMAN. Some day I'm going to swipe an image you never heard of!

Laughing, in comradely style, embraces her closely as he takes her to a seat – turning on a certain excited intimacy here.

Listen, I hitched a ride down with this pilot in his new Cessna – I have meetings up there starting seven-thirty tomorrow but I just had to astonish you.

LEAH. You flew in a small plane *at night*?

LYMAN. That whole fear was guilt, Theo – I thought I *deserved* to crash. But I deserve to live because I am not a bad guy and I love you.

THEO. Well, I'm floating away! When must you go back?

LYMAN. Now.

THEO (*near laughter at the absurdity*). Can't we even chat?

LYMAN. No. In fact, I'd better call that I'm on my way.

Goes to a point, mimes 'dialling'.

THEO. I'll drive you to the airport.

LYMAN. He's picking me up at the Carlyle . . . Hello?

LEAH *lights, holding a mimed phone.*

LEAH. Darling!

LYMAN. Be there in ten minutes.

LEAH (*puzzled*). Oh? Okay. Why are you calling?

LYMAN. Just to be sure you didn't forget me and took off.

LEAH (*a laugh at his charm*). Your jealousy is so comforting! – You know, she made a very dignified picture, reading in the window – it was like an Edward Hopper, kind of haunted.

LYMAN. Yes. Well, I'm leaving right now. (*Mimes hanging up.*)

THEO. You won't forget about dinner Thursday with Leona and Gilbert . . . he's gotten his hearing aid so it won't be so bad.

LYMAN (*with a certain solemnity, taking her hands*). – I just had to steal this extra look at one another . . . life's so stupidly short, Theo.

THEO (*happily*). Why is Death always over your shoulder? You've got more life in you than anybody! (*Ruffling his hair.*) In fact, you're kind of sparkly tonight.

LYMAN (*breathlessly*). – Listen, we have time to make love.

THEO (*a surprised, delighted laugh*). I wish I knew what's come over you!

LYMAN. That I'm alive, that's all! – I've got to have you! (*He starts to lead her.*) I keep forgetting what a sweet piece of ass my wife is!

THEO. Must be the new office in Elmira – beginnings are always exciting!

LYMAN (*turning her to him he kisses her mouth, feeling her body*). I keep meaning to ask you – has there ever been a god who was guilty?

THEO. Gods are never guilty, that's why they're gods – except Jesus, of course.

LYMAN (*kisses her reverently*). I feel like the moon's in my belly and the sun's in my mouth and I'm shining down on the world. (*Laughs with a self-mocking charm.*) . . . A regular planetary flashlight! Come!

And laughing in high tension takes her hand and moves her into darkness . . .

THEO. Oh, Lyman – how wonderfully, endlessly changing you are!

Blackout.

Light up on LEAH *in hospital room;* LYMAN *is back in his cast.*

LEAH. So you bopped her that night.

LYMAN. What can I say?

LEAH. There's just no end to you, is there? – And when you came back to the hotel, didn't we . . . ?

LYMAN. I couldn't keep myself, I was exploding with life!

Maybe it was that you were so close by, waiting for me, but she seemed absolutely gorgeous! How can that be evil?

LEAH (*a sigh*). – Listen, I have to talk business. I want the house transferred to my name immediately.

LYMAN. What are you saying? Leah . . . !

LEAH. I know how much feeling you put into it but I want the security for Benny's sake.

LYMAN. Leah, I beg you to wait with that . . .

LEAH. I will not wait with that!! And I want my business returned to me.

LYMAN. That'll be complicated – it's many times bigger than when I took it over . . .

LEAH. I want it back!! I would have expanded without you! I'm not going to be a *total* fool! I will sue you!

LYMAN. Okay, okay. Done.

LEAH (*opening her pocket book*). I don't think you'll want to get into a court just now . . .

LYMAN (*a very uncertain grin*). You'd really sue me?

LEAH (*searching in her pocketbook*). I'm not fooling around, Lyman. You've hurt me very deeply . . . (*Breaks off, holding back tears. She takes out a sheet of paper.*)

LYMAN (*forced to turn from her*). Jesus, how I hate to see you cry.

LEAH. I have something I want you to sign.

LYMAN. To *sign*?

LEAH. It's a quit-claim on the house and my business. Will you read it?

LYMAN. You're not serious.

LEAH. I had Ted Lester draw it up. Here, read it.

LYMAN. I know what a quit-claim is, don't tell me to read a quit-claim. How can you do this?

LEAH. We aren't married and I don't want you making claims on me.

LYMAN. And . . . and what about Benny. You don't mean you're taking Benny from me . . .

LEAH. I . . .

LYMAN. I want you to bring him here tomorrow morning so I can talk to him.

LEAH. Just a minute . . .

LYMAN. Now you're going to bring him, Leah . . .

LEAH. You listen to me! I've been through this with Ted Lester and you haven't a legal leg to stand on. I will not allow you to see him until I know what you intend to say to him about all this.

LYMAN. I'll tell him the truth – I love him.

LEAH. You love him.

LYMAN (*threateningly*). I said I love him, Leah!

LEAH. But what is he going to make of that? – That it's all right to deceive people you love?

LYMAN. Human beings can lose control when they fall in love, it won't hurt him to know that. You're over-protecting him.

LEAH. But how is he going to figure this out? – You love him and lied to him so terribly? – He's all I have now, Lyman, I am not going to see him go crazy!

LYMAN. Now you stop that! I did a helluva lot more than lie to him . . .

LEAH (*outpouring*). You lied to him! – Why don't you seem to register this? The whole thing was a lie!

LYMAN. I love that boy!

LEAH. . . . To buy him the pony, and teach him to ski, and take him up in the glider . . . you made him worship you – when you knew what you knew! That was cruelty!

LYMAN. All right, I won't argue. What do you think I should tell him?

LEAH. I think you have to say that you do love him but he mustn't follow your example because lying to people injures them. And you beg his pardon, and promise you'll never mislead him again.

LYMAN. I am not grinding myself up in front of my son's face! That is not education for him, kid, it's your revenge on me! And if I can teach him anything now it's to have the guts to be true to himself! That's all that matters!

LEAH. Even if he has to betray the whole world to do it?

LYMAN (*in an agony*). Only the truth is sacred, Leah! – To hold back nothing!

LEAH. You must be crazy – you held back everything! – You really don't know right from wrong, do you!

LYMAN. Jesus Christ, you sound like Theo!

LEAH. Well maybe it's what happens to people who marry you! Look – I don't think it's a good idea at the moment . . .

LYMAN. I have a right to see my son!

LEAH. I won't have him copying you, Lyman, it will destroy his life! (*She starts to leave.*)

LYMAN. I want Benny! I want Benny, Leah! You will bring me Benny!

Enter BESSIE *alone. She is extremely tense and anxious.*

BESSIE. Oh! I'm so glad you're still here. Listen . . .

LEAH. I was just going . . .

BESSIE. Please don't! She's had an attack of some kind – they're looking at her in a room down the hall.

LYMAN. My God, Bessie . . . what is it?

BESSIE. I really think it would help if she saw that you're together . . .

LEAH. But we're not together.

BESSIE. Oh! – Well, I'm not too sorry to hear that, I thought you were going to let him get away with it.

LYMAN. Well it isn't quite settled . . .

LEAH. Maybe it is, dear. (*To* BESSIE.) – What did you mean? – to see we're together?

BESSIE. – She talks about taking him home with her.

LYMAN. No kidding!

BESSIE (*a quick hostile glance at him, then . . .*). She's a little delusionary.

LEAH. Oh how awful!

BESSIE. . . . I wonder . . . if you could talk to her and tell her your feelings, maybe it would get her back to some reality about him.

LEAH. I'm sorry, dear, but I'm at the outer edge of my nervous system, I just couldn't start to . . .

LYMAN. Why must it be a delusion? Maybe Mother really wants me back . . .

BESSIE (*a frustrated stamp of her foot*). I want her out of here and home!

LYMAN. What should I do, stick horns on my head and a tail on my ass? I am not a monster, Bessie! My God, where did all this cruelty come from!

LEAH. He wants her, you see . . .

LYMAN. I want you both!

BESSIE (*with a hysterical overtone, screaming*). Will you once in your life think of another human being?

TOM and THEO enter with the NURSE; he has her by the arm. She has a heightened, 'seeing' air about her, a fixed dead smile and her head trembles.

LYMAN. Theo! – come, sit her down, Tom!

LEAH (*to BESSIE; fearfully*). I really feel I ought to go . . .

THEO. Oh, I wish you could stay a few minutes! (*To NURSE.*) Please get a chair for Mrs Felt.

The reference causes surprise in BESSIE. LEAH looks quickly to BESSIE, perplexed because this is the opposite of what she said THEO wished. LYMAN is immensely encouraged by it. The NURSE, as she goes out for the chair, glances about, perplexed.

THEO. Well! Here we are all together.

Slight pause.

TOM. She's had a little . . . incident, Lyman. (*To BESSIE.*) I've arranged for a plane; the three of us can go to the city together.

BESSIE. Oh, good. – We're ready to leave whenever you say, Mother.

LYMAN. Thanks, Theo . . . for coming.

THEO (*turns to him, smiling blankly*). Socialism is dead. (*A beat.*) And Christianity is finished, so . . . (*Searches.*) There is really nothing left to . . . to . . . Except simplicity? To defend? (*She crosses her legs, and her coat falls partially open revealing a bare thigh.*)

BESSIE. Mother! – where's your skirt?

THEO. I'm comfortable, it's all right . . .

NURSE *enters with a chair.*

BESSIE. She must have left her skirt in the room she was just in – would you get it, please?

NURSE, *perplexed again, exits.*

THEO (*to* LEAH). I wish I hadn't carried on that way . . . I'm sorry. (*Turning to* LYMAN.) The surprise is what threw me. I was just totally unprepared. But I'm better now. (*To* LEAH.) I'm really much better. (*Breaks off.*) Do you see the *Village Voice* up here?

LEAH. Yes, occasionally.

THEO. There was a strange interview some years back with Isaac Bashevis Singer, the novelist? The interviewer was a woman whose husband had left her for another woman and she couldn't understand why. And Singer said, 'Maybe he liked her hole better'. I was shocked at the time, really outraged – you know, that he'd gotten a Nobel; but now I think it was courageous to have said that, because it's probably true. Courage . . . courage is always the main thing! Everyone knows that, of course, but suddenly it is so . . . so *clear* . . .

NURSE *enters, offers her the skirt.*

NURSE. Can I help you on with it?

THEO (*takes the skirt, looks at it without recognition and drops it on the floor*). I can't remember if I called you Leah or Mrs Felt.

LEAH. I'm not really Mrs Felt.

THEO (*a pleasant social smile*). Well, it doesn't really matter – I guess we're all sort of interchangeable anyway. Except for the children. (*Short pause.*) Your boy needs his father, I imagine.

LEAH. Well . . . yes, but . . .

THEO. Then he should be here with you, shouldn't he? (*To* LYMAN.) You can come up here whenever you want to . . . if that's what you'd like to do.

BESSIE (*to* TOM). She's really too ill for this. – Come, Mother, we're going . . .

THEO (*to* LYMAN). I can say 'fuck', you know. I never cared for the word but I'm sure she has her limitations too. I can say 'fuck me', 'fuck you'; whatever.

LYMAN *is silent in guilty anguish.*

BESSIE (*to* LYMAN, *furiously*). Will you tell her to leave? – Just out of respect, out of friendship!

LYMAN. Yes. (*Delicately.*) She's right, Theo, I think that would be the best . . .

THEO (*to* BESSIE). No, I can take better care of him at home. (*To* LEAH.) I really have nothing to do, and you're busy, I imagine . . .

BESSIE. Tom, will you . . . ?

TOM. Why don't we let her say what's on her mind?

THEO (*to* BESSIE). He had every right to resent me. What did I ever do but correct him? (*To* LEAH.) You don't correct him, do you. You like him as he is, even now, don't you. And that's the secret, isn't it. (*To* LYMAN.) Well I can do that. I don't need to correct you . . . or rather pretend to . . .

BESSIE. I can't bear this, Mother!

THEO (*calmly to* BESSIE). But Bessie dear, I've always pretty well known what he was doing. I think I have, anyway; why have I tolerated it? (*Suddenly screams at the top of her lungs.*) Why have I tolerated it!

Silence. Fear in all of them.

BESSIE (*terrified for her mother*). Daddy, please . . . tell her . . . ?

LYMAN. But she's trying to tell the truth, darling.

LEAH (*suddenly filling up*). You poor woman! (*To him.*) – What a bastard you are; one honest sentence from you and none of this would have happened, it's despicable! (*Appealing to* THEO.) I'm so sorry about it, Mrs Felt . . .

THEO. No-no . . . he's absolutely right – he's always said

it – it's life I can't bear! But you accept it, you trust it, and that's why you *should* win out . . .

LEAH. But it's not true – I never really trusted him! Not really! Not really *trusted*. To tell you the truth, I never wanted to marry anybody, I've never known one happy couple! – Listen, you mustn't blame yourself, the whole damned thing doesn't work, it never works . . . which I knew and went ahead and did it anyway and I'll never understand why!

LYMAN (*bitter anger*). Because if you hadn't married me you wouldn't have kept Benny. Don't start being a dumb-bell, Leah!

She can't find words.

– You wouldn't have had Benny or this last nine years of your happiness. You've become the woman you always wanted to be, instead of . . . (*Catches himself.*) Well, what's the difference?

LEAH. No, don't stop – instead of what? What did you save me from?

LYMAN (*accepting her challenge*). All right . . . from all those lonely post-coital showerbaths, and the pointless pillow talk and the boxes of heartless condoms beside your bed . . .

LEAH (*speechless*). Well now!

LYMAN. I'm sick of this crap, Leah! – You got a little something out of this despicable treachery!

THEO. That's a terrible thing to say to the woman.

LYMAN. But the truth is terrible, isn't that what you've just finished saying? Are you still looking for your purity, Theo? You tolerated me because you loved me, and more than I deserved, but wasn't it also the good life I gave you. – Well, what's wrong with that? Aren't women people? Don't people love power? I don't understand the disgrace!

BESSIE (*to both women*). Why are you still sitting here, don't you have any pride! – (*To* LEAH.) This is disgusting!

LEAH. Will you please stop challenging everybody? I have

business with him, so I have to talk to him! – I'll go out of my mind here! Am I being accused of something?

BESSIE. You shouldn't be in the same room with him!

LEAH (*rattled*). I just explained that, didn't I? *What the hell do you want!*

LYMAN (*through a cry*). She wants her father back!

BESSIE. You son of a bitch! (*Raises her fists, then weeps helplessly.*)

LYMAN. I love you, Bessie! – All of you! You are all magnificent!

BESSIE. You ought to be killed!

She bursts into tears. A helpless river of grief which now overflows to sweep up LYMAN; *then* LEAH *is carried away by the wave of weeping. All strategies collapse as finally* THEO *is infected. The four of them are helplessly covering their faces. It is a veritable mass keening, a funerary explosion of grief, each for his or her own condition, for love's frustration and for the end of all their capacity to reason.*

TOM *has turned from them, head bent in prayer, hands clasped, eyes shut.*

LYMAN. Theo, please! – Put some clothes on! (*Turning for help to* TOM.) Tom, I can't bear her doing this. . . ! (*Breaks off.*) Are you praying, for Christ's sake?

TOM (*staring ahead, only glancing at them*). There is no way to go forward. You must all stop loving him. You must, or he will destroy you. He is an endless string attached to nothing. – Theo needs help now, Lyman, and I don't want a conflict, so I don't see how I can go on representing you.

LYMAN. – Why? Am I not worthy? Who is not an endless string? (*A shout, but with the strain of his loss, his inability to connect.*) Who is attached to something in this world now? – I am human, I am proud of it! – Of the glory and the shit!

TOM. You must face it, Lyman, you moved that barrier . . .

LYMAN. That was not suicide – I am not a cop-out!

TOM. Why is it a cop-out to have a conscience? You were ashamed, weren't you? Why can't you acknowledge that? Isn't a conscience human? Your shame is the best part of you, for God's sake . . . ! (*Breaks off, giving it up.*) – I'm ready to go, Theo.

LYMAN. Let her stay a while. (*To* THEO.) You want to stay, don't you?

BESSIE. Mother? (*She raises* THEO *to her feet. Her head is trembling. She turns to* LYMAN.)

LYMAN. You can't really leave me, Theo – you can't!

THEO. I'm afraid I have nothing . . . in me any more, Lyman.

BESSIE *takes her by the arm to go.* LEAH *stands, as though to leave.*

LYMAN. – Bessie? I'll see you again, won't I? – Some time?

BESSIE *is silent.*

Leah? – You can stay a little, can't you?

LEAH (*an evasive colour*). I have work in the office . . .

LYMAN (*with a scared laugh*). You all pulling out? – What is this?

LEAH. I'll try to stop by tomorrow, if I can . . .

LYMAN (*open terror at her cool tone*). I want you to bring Benny.

LEAH. . . . I can't, it's a school day . . .

LYMAN (*terrified*). You're not taking Benny from me?

She can't answer.

You bring Benny to me, Leah!

FATHER *appears, shaking out his black shroud. They are all moving to leave.*

LEAH. Stop shouting! – I can't bring him!

FATHER *flaps out the shroud which billows out before him.* LYMAN's *fear rises.*

LYMAN. Don't leave me like this, for Christ's sake! (*They continue moving; he is terrified.*) I said wait a minute . . . ! Don't leave me, Leah, Bessie . . . Theo, listen . . . !

With a sudden billowing movement, FATHER *sweeps the black cloth billowing out over* LYMAN *on the bed, covering him completely. He shouts from underneath . . .*

No! Don't! Pa! Please! Don't do it!

LEAH. Stop this! Why are you yelling!

LYMAN (*thrashing around in terror*). Where's the light! Where is the fucking light!

LEAH (*to* TOM *for help*). What is he doing?

LYMAN *flings off the shroud, still terrified – all they see is that he has been thrashing about; and he lies there now panting for breath as* FATHER *walks into darkness trailing the shroud, muttering.*

LEAH (*starts away swiftly*). I can't bear it any more!

LYMAN (*a look of amazement*). Wait! Wait, please . . . I remember what happened! – How I got on the mountain! (*As memory floods back.*) – I kept calling you from the Howard Johnson's – yes. To tell you I'd be staying over because of the storm . . . but the line was busy. So I went to bed, yes . . . But it was still busy . . . over an hour . . . more! And I . . . yes, I started to ask the operator to cut in as an emergency, but . . . (*Breaks off.*) I remembered something you once said to me . . .

LEAH. I was talking to . . .

LYMAN (*quick fury*). I'm telling you what *happened*! – Let me finish!

LEAH. I was talking to my brother!

LYMAN. In Japan, for over an hour?

LEAH. He just got back on Monday.

LYMAN. Well, it doesn't matter.

LEAH. It certainly does matter!

LYMAN. Leah, remember you once said . . . 'I might lie to you,' remember that? Way at the beginning? It seemed so wonderful then . . . that you could be so honest; but now, on my back in that room, I started to die.

LEAH (*outraged*). I said it was my brother!

LYMAN. You're not understanding me, I'm not blaming you. I got dressed and back in the car to . . . *feel something again*. 'Cause it had all died in me, Leah – this whole ten-year commute was just . . . ludicrous! I was a corpse buried in that room; I couldn't wait . . . (*A laugh at himself.*) I know it was crazy but I thought if I walked in two-three in the morning out of a roaring blizzard like that . . . you'd be so amazed, you'd believe how I needed you . . . *and I would believe it too!* (*Near weeping.*) And maybe we'd really fall in love again.

LEAH (*covering her face, weeping*). Oh God, Lyman . . . !

He looks at them standing there in their desolation.

LYMAN. I got back in the car to stop the dying. So I know the suffering I've been for you, I tried not to but I do see it now.

Looks from one to the other; there is no agreement from them.

Then all I am is shit? Is that the last word?

But no one answers or moves.

. . . I don't understand it, do I?

No one moves.

(*Outcry.*) Help me, Bessie, what is it? What should I understand!

BESSIE. There are other people.

A long pause.

LYMAN (*staring ahead*). Yes. That's as simple as an arrow, darling. (*With a soberly wondrous acceptance.*) Okay. (*Pause.*) But I have known what love feels like, darling; for you I could give my life without a second thought. – But probably not for anybody else, so I know what you're trying to tell me, dear girl. (*He looks at them all.*) It's okay – if you want to go now. It's over.

BESSIE turns away to shield her feelings.

But I have to say this – in some miserable dark corner of my soul I'm still not sure why I'm condemned.

They don't move; he goes perfectly still. And now with dread.

Are you hearing me? Are you in this room!

BESSIE. Come, Mother.

She smooths THEO's hair – her head is in noticeable tremor.

THEO. . . . Say goodbye to him, dear.
BESSIE (*dry-eyed now; her feeling clearer, she has a close to impersonal sound*). I hope you're better soon, Daddy. Goodbye.

She takes her mother's arm – THEO no longer resists as they move out into darkness. He turns to LEAH.

LYMAN. Oh Leah, say something tough and honest . . . the way you can.
LEAH. I don't know if I'll ever believe anything . . . or anybody, again.
LYMAN. Oh no. No! – I haven't done that!

A great weeping sweeps her and she rushes out.

LYMAN. Leah! *Leah!*

But she is gone.

TOM. Talk to you soon.

He sees that LYMAN is lost in space, and he goes out. The NURSE comes from her corner to him.

NURSE. You got pain?

He doesn't reply.

I'll get you something to smooth you out.

LYMAN. Don't leave me alone, okay? – For a little while? Please. Sit with me. (*Pats the mattress.*) Come, don't be afraid.

She approaches the bed reluctantly; he draws her down to sit beside him. He takes her hand.

It's just two worlds, see? – Women want it safe, but it's dangerous. Just is. Can't help it. It's terrible. And it's okay.

NURSE (*not giving agreement*). Let me get you something. (*Starts to withdraw her hand.*)

LYMAN (*holding onto her hand*). Ten more seconds – I love your warmth, Hogan. A woman's warmth is the last sacredness; you're a piece of the sun. The last magic. – Which reminds me . . . When you're out there fishing on the ice with your husband and your boy . . . what do you talk about?

NURSE. . . . Well, let's see . . . this last time we all bought us some shoes at that big Knapp Shoe Outlet up there? – They're seconds, but you can't tell them from new.

LYMAN. So you talked about your new shoes?

NURSE. Well they're great buys.

LYMAN. Right. That . . . that's just wonderful to do that. I don't know why, but it just is.

NURSE. I'll be right back.

She starts away.

LYMAN. Hate me?

NURSE (*an embarrassed shrug*). I don't know. I got to think about it.

LYMAN. Come right back, huh? I'm still a little . . . shaky.

She leans down and kisses his forehead.

Why'd you do that?

NURSE. No reason.

She exits.

LYMAN (*painful wonder and longing in his face, his eyes wide, alive . . .*). What a miracle everything is! Absolutely everything! . . . Imagine . . . three of them sitting out there together on that lake, talking about their shoes!

He begins to weep.

Blackout.

Almost Everybody Wins

A Screenplay

Author's Note

The passage of time does wonders for a perspective on past labours. Over a decade ago I wrote this screenplay, later produced as *Everybody Wins*, with Debra Winger and Nick Nolte. It was based on a one-act play of mine called *Some Kind of Love Story*, performed at the Young Vic in a marvellously directed production by David Thacker, with Helen Mirren and Robert Peck.

Now, twelve years after writing this screenplay, it seems a shame that I helped change it from what I believe could have been a wonderfully ironic and funny film into a fairly interesting one. In the original script printed here, the woman, Angela, has a personality split into quite separate parts. Tom the detective, in trying to unearth whatever shreds of truth might be shuttling from one of her personalities to the other is driven half mad trying to figure out when she is fantasizing, when she is lying outright, and when she is being truthful – or more or less so. In the course of production Angela's character lost its various personas and her fantastic quality and she ended up merely a terrified woman who dares not reveal what she knows about a frightful murder.

For better or worse – I am still not sure which – the present script is built as much on language as on visualization, while the balance of the finished film leaned far more toward the pictorial. Naturally, I prefer this version for reasons both subjective and the other kind.

Arthur Miller
1995

Characters

ANGELA CRISPINI
TOM O'TOOLE
CONNIE
JOHN CALLAGHAN
JUDGE HARRY MARKS
FELIX
JERRY
AMY
ROBIE
SONNY
MONTANA
BELLANCA
JUDGE
DEFENSE ATTORNEY
FATHER MANCINI
DR LEVY
MRS HEARST
JEAN
INTERVIEWER
LOBBY-MAN
GUARDS, COPS

Exterior: Day

*We are introduced to Minorville – at least to its surface aspects –
through the window of a moving car. It is a New England city of
perhaps 100,000 in the fall of the year. The white colonial church
speaks of order and goodness, and the surrounding Victorian
houses seem untouched by our century. Peaceful scenes flow past –
the neat schoolyard and kids playing; the firehouse with gleaming
machines within or being polished out front, and so on. Now a
different aspect – rows of rents, two or three-storey wooden
buildings with outside stairways; decayed stores and a few
loungers out on the streets; and a bridge across a river from which
we see both the lovely tree-lined shores and one or two immense
abandoned mills with hundreds of windows, many of them
smashed. And now Main Street with some ambitiously modern
storefronts alongside the undistinguished and corny and decayed.*

Few shoppers are out at mid-morning.

*We move in a nondescript, working-class neighborhood and come
to a stop before a house.* TOM O'TOOLE *leaves the car and
compares the house number with one he has jotted on a slip of
paper, rings the bell, waits, looking up and down the quiet street.
He is in his forties, dressed in a small-town way, in a knee-length
reversible and porkpie hat.*

*He rings again, looking up at the windows; looks at his watch,
shakes his head in anger at himself as well as the human race for
this waste of his time, starts back to his car in a beginning
temper . . .*

ANGELA, *heels rapping, comes running up the street to him,
already waving. She is chronologically over the hill, perhaps, but
only chronologically. A low-cut dress, makeup too heavy for the*

*morning, high heels, and an incongruous attaché case in one hand
and a fresh newspaper in the other. She is breathless.*

ANGELA. You're right on time! Hi!

She holds out her hand, he shakes it, somewhat thrown off.

You're even handsomer than your pictures, aren't you.
But I'd know you in a minute. Can we go? – Sorry, but I
had to run around and pick up my *New York Times* . . .
they only get three a day in this whole town! (*Indicates
car.*) Okay?

TOM (*recovering from this barrage*). I think you must've
misunderstood, Mrs Crispini. I only agreed to talk about
the case with you today . . .

ANGELA. Oh my God . . . ! But I already told him you're
coming! What happened? I sent you the transcript . . .

TOM. I mailed it back to you, I read it. But I told you when
you called . . . I'd be glad to talk about it and be of any
help I can but I don't know if I want to start a whole new
case . . .

ANGELA. I didn't sleep all night just thinkin' about him
meetin' you today . . . 'cause he gets so discouraged, you
know?

TOM. Well, I'm sorry if I . . .

ANGELA (*a new idea*). Listen – Let me show you something
upstairs . . . (*Tugging his sleeve.*) Two minutes! Just to
show you what I think of you! – and not just lately!

*Before he can demur she is rattling up the stoop and into the
house and he follows, intrigued but not unworried.*

Interior: ANGELA's *apartment – Day*

*The room is a mess, an amazing profusion of bras, underwear,
skirts, blouses, shoes – she has probably tried on her whole stock
and dropped it on the run before meeting him.*

She is just slipping a cassette into her VCR.

ANGELA. You probably won't even remember this . . . the day you got the reversal on the baby Schmidlap case?

TV screen: TOM, PROSECUTOR CALLAGHAN – *Courthouse steps. A TV news* INTERVIEWER *has a mike up to* TOM's *face. He is glancing with highly pleasurable irony toward State's Prosecutor* CALLAGHAN, *who stands there trying not to explode.*

INTERVIEWER. How do you feel about this victory, Mr O'Toole?

TOM. Frankly, superb; but of course, getting reversals of a prosecutor's case is not all that unusual – I mean in this particular jurisdiction.

INTERVIEWER. And you, Mr Callaghan?

CALLAGHAN (*a rather preppy type, but tough and intelligent and nattily dressed; about forty, probably reddish, nicely barbered hair*). I intend to try the defendant again and you can be sure he will be convicted again, and of course the public will pay the costs again. I regret very much that we have come to where so-called private investigators can shoot down the verdicts of faithful, hard-working juries and make a travesty of our whole system of justice!

ANGELA *shuts off the machine.*

TOM (*immensely excited – flattered*). What're you doing with that?

ANGELA. Can I tell you in the car? Felix is really expecting us!

He opens his mouth to resist again, but the will to do so has weakened before her insistence and the simple fact that she has opened the door and is standing there winsomely – and wittily – asking . . .

Please?

Interior: TOM's *car – Day*

The car is several years old and has never been washed.

ANGELA. Can I call you Tom?

TOM. Sure!

ANGELA. Then you can stop calling me Mrs Crispini.

He drives through town, heading for the interstate. She takes out a cigarette, holds it for a moment, then returns it to the pack.

Anyway, I'm really a Finn. (*Slight pause.*) Which is not the same as a Swede. 'Cause you might hear people calling me 'the Swede'. (*Slight pause.*) Not that I was ever in Finland.

TOM *simply nods and grunts, glancing at her in fascination and puzzlement.*

I just can't believe I'm actually sitting next to you! I mean, to me, – rea<u>d</u>ing about you the last few years, and seeing you on TV fighting for people like that . . . (*Turning to him, confessionally.*) . . . I might as well say it – to me, if there is such a thing as hope for the world, a man like you is it.

TOM (*embarrassed laugh*). Wish I could say the same – Incidentally, what's your connection with this case?

ANGELA. In a few words?

She is thoughtful for a moment, rapt, eagerly tense, trying to formulate a complicated thought . . . then gives up . . .

We'll have to sit down; . . . I mean it's very compli- cated . . .

She draws a cigarette out and holds it, puts it between her lips, then returns it to the pack.

TOM. Don't you ever light them?

ANGELA. I'm bustin' my nuts trying to quit. So I go through the motions. Everything in the world is suggestion, you know – like one step away from a dream.

TOM (*mystified, yet drawn on*). It sure feels like it sometimes.

ANGELA. Like I had this doctor telling me I had a cancer.

TOM. You're kiddin'.

ANGELA. But I don't.

TOM (*impressed*). How do you know?

ANGELA. Because. From the day I made up my mind, the pains stopped.

TOM. No kiddin'!

ANGELA. But of course I completely gave up alcohol. And sex.

TOM. No kiddin'!!

ANGELA. You don't think it's possible?

TOM. Listen, the way you look I'd have to doubt it, but . . . I know it's *possible*.

ANGELA (*eyes him with surprise*). Can I ask what you mean by that?

TOM. What I said.

ANGELA. But why sex?

TOM (*blushing, but something about her liberates his feelings*). I don't know . . . the usual, I guess – sooner or later Mother Nature starts to let you down.

ANGELA. Really. At your age. It's purified me completely, I never felt . . . you know . . . this clean.

TOM. Well, that's good. I have sort of mixed feelings about it myself.

He ducks to look up at a gate guard, who recognizes him and waves him through.

Interior: Visitors' room, Penitentiary – Soon after

TOM *and* ANGELA *are seating themselves in two adjoining chairs that face a long table, dividing the room. The guard gives her a lusty glance and a super-appreciative gesture to* TOM, *who seems a bit embarrassed by it, but proud, too, of his implicit distinction. Guard leaves.*

ANGELA. Boy, you are great-looking! (*Now intimately.*) It's so important you came – see, his appeal comes up on Thursday . . .

TOM. On what grounds?

ANGELA. Well, we're claiming his lawyer was incompetent, see.

TOM. That's not very good grounds.

ANGELA (*searching in her attaché case*). I know – so if we lose the appeal, it's very important he should feel something else is being done, y'see?

TOM. Hold it, will you? I'd have to study the case a lot more before I commit myself . . .

ANGELA. I want to show you what he looked like when they arrested him. You're not going to believe this.

She searches in her attaché case.

TOM. Y'know, I still don't dig your connection – did you say you didn't know him before the murder . . . ?

ANGELA. Oh no, I never knew Felix till the trial. But Abe had been my doctor.

TOM. Abe . . . oh, you mean the man who was killed.

ANGELA. Dr Daniels. Didn't I mention that? He'd been a very wonderful friend to me. So I started attending the trial.

TOM. Oh! Well, now I understand.

ANGELA. It got me so upset I couldn't sleep. I mean, to listen to that Callaghan going on day after day about absolutely zero . . . he had no evidence!

TOM. I may as well tell you; John Callaghan is the one big reason I even returned your call. You know, he's tried to get my investigator's license revoked, damn near put me out of business.

ANGELA. Please don't talk to me about John Callaghan because I get so upset I can't . . .

She realizes she has a newspaper clipping in her hand.

Oh . . . here's Felix. When they arrested him. Look at that man.

TOM *takes the clipping.*

Close-up: Photo of FELIX. *He is a conventionally dapper man in his late thirties, successful, topcoat over his arm, hat in hand.*

Interior: Visitors' room – Same time

Guard enters first, followed by FELIX. TOM *and* ANGELA *stand.* FELIX *now has a head of straggly white hair, a long white beard and haunted, frightened eyes, and stands a bit bent. He seems a recluse living under a rock. Guard leaves.* ANGELA *approaches* FELIX *delicately, unsure whether he even recognizes her.* TOM *is immediately quite moved, but not swept away.*

ANGELA. Hello, dear . . . It's Angela. You remember.
FELIX. . . . You came back?
ANGELA. I always come back, dear! I brought Mr O'Toole, *Tom* O'Toole, remember? – On TV when he got the reversal on the Baby Schmidlap case?

FELIX *stares at* TOM, *undecided.*

TOM. Whyn't we sit down, Mr Epstein?

As they do – ANGELA *nurses* FELIX *into a chair.*

ANGELA. You don't look like you're eating, Felix.
FELIX (*to* ANGELA). Terrible class of people in here.
ANGELA. But you have to eat.
FELIX. They cook everything in antiseptic.

TOM *clears his throat.*

TOM (*taking charge*). If you don't mind, Felix; I understand you live in Boston – how'd you come to be all the way down in Minorville the night your uncle was killed?
FELIX (*stares*). For the thousandth time – I wanted to talk to

him about putting up for a mortgage on my shopping mall, which I was building in the River Basin area up there.

TOM. But why that night in particular? – a weekend and all?

FELIX (*against a threatening upsurge of anger against himself*). Because my ex-girlfriend, Martha Solomon lives in Minorville and she agreed to have dinner on Saturday night – is that some kind of crime that we might get together again?

TOM. But there's no mention of your date in the transcript . . .

Suddenly FELIX'*s sleepiness is gone and he is crying out.*

FELIX. Because my lawyer was such a big shot intellectual schmuck who wouldn't be bothered to call her in! That man destroyed me! Lunchtime he's reading poetry instead of thinking! And twenty-five thousand dollars he took for that!

ANGELA. Ssh! Everything's going to change now, dear.

TOM (*lets him subside*). Felix, can you tell me . . . what's the first notification you had of your uncle being murdered?

FELIX. I read it in the paper – he's cut up like a chicken in his living room. I nearly fainted!

TOM. And what next?

FELIX. . . . Two days later a couple of Boston detectives come into my office – 'Can we look at your comb?' 'My comb? Sure.' I take it out of my pocket. They leave, and next day, I am under arrest. I have to tell you, Mr O'Toole, this woman has been wonderful, but I am not in this world any more – I am walking around, but I'm dead. I'm not crazy yet, you understand, but I'm . . . I . . .

He weeps softly. ANGELA *gives* TOM *a 'you-see-how-innocent-he-is' look, but* TOM *resists sentiment.*

TOM. I'd like you to listen. – Felix?

ANGELA. Felix, listen to him, dear, he's wonderful.

TOM. In your uncle's house that night, can you remember? – did you comb your hair?

FELIX. I've been over that a thousand times . . . I'm talking to him about investing a hundred thousand dollars, how do I come to start combing my hair?

TOM. How about in the bathroom? You'd just had dinner with your date, right? Didn't you have to go to the bathroom?

FELIX. Say, now . . . That's right, I remember there were gold faucets.

TOM. And you used to be a pretty neat dresser, right? – wouldn't you have combed your hair in there?

FELIX. But they found the broken tooth of my comb in the living room, it was right next to the bodies.

TOM. Not according to their first report. Only days later, on a second search, they miraculously find the tooth of your comb on the carpet next to where the bodies were.

FELIX. You mean it was moved there?

ANGELA (*points at* TOM: *to* FELIX). What'd I tell you!

TOM (*abruptly*). Well, it was nice meeting you, Felix – I'll be thinking about it and if I come up with any ideas I'll be in touch with Mrs Crispini. Take care now . . .

He turns to ANGELA, *but she is gone from her chair; he looks around and sees her standing by a window, gets up and goes to her. A remarkably intense look is upon her; she seems elevated, a seer and at the same time somehow sensually charged up. She turns to him and whispers.*

ANGELA. My God! Your face . . . you suddenly looked like the sun shooting out lights . . . You've got to take this case, you were born for this!

TOM (*put off and drawn in as well by her strange intensity*). Let me think about it. I don't know . . .

Interior: Courtroom – Day

It is all from TOM's *viewpoint: he is seated at the back of the courtroom, observing as the* DEFENSE ATTORNEY *is concluding his appeal to the Bench, while* PROSECUTOR CALLAGHAN *waits his turn. Chief of Detectives* BELLANCA *looks on from* CALLAGHAN'S *side.*

ANGELA *sits in another part of the room, attaché case on her lap, pad and pencil at the ready.*

DEFENSE ATTORNEY. It comes down, Your Honor, to the perfectly obvious fact that Felix Epstein did not have competent counsel, and we appeal to the court for a new trial.

JUDGE. Mr Callaghan?

CALLAGHAN. Your Honor, defendant's counsel was very successful in numerous other cases; he is a well-known attorney with a reputable law firm. Epstein was convicted of a bloody and brutal murder; there is not the slightest doubt about his guilt . . .

ANGELA *violently shakes her head, 'No!'*

. . . the evidence is damning and complete. This appeal has absolutely no basis in fact; the State asks that it be denied.

TOM *observes that* CALLAGHAN *has shot a glance toward* ANGELA, *but its meaning is not clear to him – does he know her or is it simply that he suddenly noticed a strange woman in the empty courtroom?*

JUDGE (*turns down to the* DEFENSE ATTORNEY). Defendant's appeal for a new trial is denied.

Interior: Courthouse corridor – Later

TOM *and* ANGELA *are about to turn a corner in the corridor when they nearly run into* CALLAGHAN, *who engraves a wide grin onto his face. He seems not to have noticed* ANGELA *at all . . . he keeps moving.*

CALLAGHAN. O'Toole! – what brings you here! – I haven't
seen any cameras.

TOM (*with a wry grin holds up a finger*). Wait!

They both are angrily intense and affect to laugh – CALLAGHAN
throws an unreadably blind glance at ANGELA *as he turns and
walks away.*

Exterior: ANGELA's *block – Night*

*Her street. Wooden three-storey 'rents' – not a slum, but working-
class definitely.* TOM's *car pulls up before her house, in which no
lights shine.*

Interior: TOM's *car – Same time*

She is opening her door; he is looking ahead; she lingers.

ANGELA. So where would you say we are? – Could I ask you
up for a minute?

TOM. I've got a court appearance first thing in the morning, I
better hit the pike.

ANGELA. . . . I'm really scared what Felix might do when he
hears the appeal's been turned down. – And incidentally,
he's not poor, you know, you'd get paid.

TOM. That'd be nice, how about you?

ANGELA. Me!

TOM. I'm sorry, kid, but I still don't dig your connection –
what's this all about?

ANGELA. Look, I can't talk here. (*With a mixture of seductive-
ness and some unexplained fear she grips his arm, smiling
wittily . . .*) Come up, will you? I get so little chance to
talk to anyone who isn't stepping on his own fingers . . . I
mean, Christ, you look like a *man*!

TOM (*laughs, flattered*). Hey, gimme a break, will ya?

ANGELA. Please!

TOM (*serious now*). I don't understand why they would want to frame Felix. Do you?

ANGELA. They're watching.

TOM (*juices flow*). Who's watching?

ANGELA. On the corner. Cops.

He turns to look up the street, then down the other direction.

They just pulled out.

Her fear is so palpable that as she gets out of the car he gets out, too, and they head to her door.

TOM. You sure? I didn't see anybody.

With hand shaking, she works her key nervously in the lock. He helps insert the key with a steady hand.

Interior: ANGELA's *apartment – Moments later*

The living room is practically bare with no personality of the owner. Everything is neat as if the room is never used.

ANGELA. Lock the door, will ya?

TOM *does – three locks and a safety chain.*

ANGELA *calls from the bedroom.*

Come on in.

Interior: Bedroom – Same time

TOM *enters the bedroom; this time he has a moment to examine it. It is a crowded, intensely lived-in, cavelike room. He observes* ANGELA *neatening up, scooping up the debris of underwear, bras, stockings, skirts, blouses, shoes that are scattered everywhere.*

ANGELA. Be with you in a second . . . would you like some vitamins?

TOM. Use your phone?

ANGELA. Sure!

She swings the door of the bathroom open and goes in, closing it behind her. He picks up the phone beside her bed and dials.

TOM. Me, Connie. I'll be leavin' in a couple of minutes. No-no, I'm stayin' out of it. – I don't know, I suppose Epstein could've done it, but I have to admit there is a slightly putrid smell about it. – Well, John Callaghan was the prosecutor, need I say more? Fifteen years ago I'd have gone after it, but I'm tired, kid. – Now? I'm waitin' for the woman to come out of the bathroom so I can give her my opinion, why? – I said I'm not gettin' into it, what do you want, a signed contract!! Why should I be mad . . . Do I sound mad?

He hangs up, furious, but it quickly subsides. He is sitting in a boudoir-type armchair. Looks about the room – the rumpled bed, covered with a satin throw, worn carpet, Grand Rapids Baroque plastic-tufted headboard . . . and finally he spots a surprising shelf of books, walks over to inspect the titles. And under it, a kind of drape which is partly open, revealing, once he gently moves it completely aside, an oak double-drawer filing cabinet. A heavy padlock has been affixed to the drawers. He lets the drape fall closed again.

ANGELA *enters.*

ANGELA. Well! This is better!

She is in a very nearly transparent negligee, which forces him instinctively to glance down and away.

TOM (*with nearly a snigger of laughter*). Boy, that's quite a little outfit there.

ANGELA (*stretching onto the bed*). Like some herb tea?

TOM. No, I'm fine. Now listen . . .

As much to ward off her incitation as anything else, he sits on the edge of the chair, looking very businesslike.

ANGELA (*openly stretching the moment*). What's this case you're on?

TOM. Nothing important. I work for insurance companies occasionally, pick up some easy bread.

ANGELA. That must be very interesting.

TOM. Molto boring. I run checks on executives they're thinking of promoting. This one's gonna be made Vice-President of a ball-bearin' company and they want to know if he's gay.

ANGELA. Jeeze, they still doin' that?

TOM. Well, you can't have a homosexual Vice-President of a ball-bearin' company. (*Shifts, about to rise.*) Maybe, I'll see you around – go into this further sometime.

ANGELA. There's a lot bigger case here than meets the eye, Tom.

TOM (*already loath to lose contact, equivocally*). Maybe you better not tell me.

ANGELA. I guess so, if you're staying out of it . . . You're breaking my heart, y'know.

TOM. Tell you the truth, it's got that old familiar stink, but I really can't see myself goin' up against the system again. I just don't have it any more.

ANGELA. Can I tell you the reason I called you? – Because the man who does this case is going to need a pair of brass balls, which I happen to know is what you've got.

TOM (*flattered*). I know, kid, but the time comes when you realize the public has to love corruption or you wouldn't have crooked judges fallin' out of the trees every ten minutes, and they wouldn't be electing unscrupulous meatheads like John Callaghan to run the criminal justice system . . .

ANGELA. You're a thrill just to listen to. I mean you're the only one who can talk about something else besides money and pussy.

TOM. Well, I couldn't resist my curiosity, bein' it's a John Callaghan case, but let me maul it over some more.

(*Stands. Holds out his hand.*) Take care, and it was terrific
meetin' you . . .

ANGELA. I know the murderer.

TOM (*it stops him cold, but he tries to remain cool and skeptically
apart*). Yeah?

The issue is her credibility and she stares him right in the eye.

That raises a number of questions, doesn't it.

ANGELA. Oh, the cops know who it is. In fact, they had him
and let him go.

TOM. You knew this when they were trying Felix?

ANGELA. There was no way I could say anything.

TOM (*postponing*). . . . Right. But now?

ANGELA. I'm ready to talk. But there's a couple of things I
still need to prove; that's why I need you. Felix is the tip of
the iceberg, this case goes to the top of the criminal justice
system. (*Pats her mattress as she stretches out on the bed.*)
God, I'm exhausted . . . could you sit just a minute before
you go?

He sits beside her on the bed.

You mind if I touch your hand?

TOM. Don't try to crank me up, kid, you'll only get tired.

ANGELA. I talk better when I'm touching . . . According to
that interview you got nuns in the family?

TOM. A sister and two brothers priests. But it never rubbed
off.

ANGELA. I'm more into it since my cancer scare – I have a
friend, Father Mancini at Saint Jude's?

TOM. Don't know him.

*Her sensuality toward him is becoming unabashed, and he sees
it plainly and is aroused.*

ANGELA. When I told him my feelings about you, – the kind
of fighter you are – he said, 'God places certain people on

the earth to fight for truth and justice.' He thinks you're
one. And I'm another. You mind if I kiss you?

*Before he can react she is drawing him down and kissing him
. . . rather chastely, temptingly.*

You could wrap up the case in a month – I know what to
look for and where to look.

Her hand moves down his body; he is exploding with surprise.

Hey! – what's this about Mother Nature lettin' you down!

He is on her with ravishing happiness.

Interior: TOM's *bathroom – Night*

*He is just slipping on his pyjama top and stares at himself in the
mirror – he admires himself as though he has just discovered his
attractiveness.*

*But as he turns to go out his eyes show his mystification and guilt.
He opens the door and goes into his bedroom where his lover*
CONNIE *is sitting up in bed. A high-school teacher, she is
correcting a small pile of papers resting on the blanket beside her.*

CONNIE. She sounds ditsy to me.

TOM. I would prefer librarians, but they rarely know where
the bodies are buried.

CONNIE. But you don't even know who she is or her
connection to the case.

TOM (*picking up one of the papers*). I've got a gut feeling, that's
all. There's a quagmire under this thing a mile deep. –
What's this word supposed to be?

CONNIE (*a glance at the paper he is pointing to*). 'Apparently.'

TOM. 'A-p-o-r-o-n-d-l-y?'

CONNIE. It's creative spelling. But he's captain of the
swimming team.

TOM. He'd better be. I don't know how you can go on trying to teach anything to these clucks.

CONNIE. I concentrate on the good ones – (*Shyly, but determined to underline this.*) We've all got to accentuate the postive, don't we? – I mean, that's life.

TOM. Right. (*Takes a book off the nightstand, opens it. Embarrassed.*) I can't always do what I'd like to, Connie.

CONNIE. I know. (*Puts down her papers.*) I'm here when you're ready.

He touches her hand thankfully, full of conflict.

– I thought you weren't going to take on any more long criminal cases.

TOM. Connie . . . the woman claims Callaghan convicted an innocent man –

CONNIE. But if she knows the murderer why doesn't she just come out and tell you?

TOM. Darlin', please, the woman is scared, that's understandable . . .

CONNIE (*affecting amusement*). She really got you going, didn't she . . .

TOM. What are you talking about . . . ?

CONNIE. Good night, dear.

She turns on her side, closes her eyes. He stares ahead in turmoil, mystified. Phone rings. Shocked, he picks it up as CONNIE half rises.

TOM (*into phone*). Yeah? . . . Oh, hya!

She witnesses the excitement flaring in his face.

Now? I'm an hour away, I'm in bed! . . . Well, good, I'm glad you feel that way about it . . . Right, talk to you in the morning. 'Night.

He hangs up. He sees the anxiety and incipient jealousy in CONNIE's face; his only hope is to ignore it.

Exterior: Country road – Day

His car proceeding slowly on a narrow dirt road. It stops as a motorcyclist comes zooming out of the brush beside the road – this is JERRY, *but* TOM *barely gets a glimpse of his face before he disappears up the road.* TOM *gets out and turns to look down a dirt driveway leading to a gloomy, small house, surrounded by trees and brush. He starts up the driveway. A shot. He halts. Second shot. He steps behind a tree and looks.*

TOM's *point of view: In front of the house, a stringy young woman, wearing jeans and a bandanna and a man's coat is just lowering a shotgun, which is pointed off camera, not at* TOM.

Exterior: AMY's *house – Same time*

TOM *steps from behind the tree* . . .

TOM. Excuse me . . .

   AMY *screams in shock, drops the gun, paralyzed. He approaches her. She is drug-pale.*

   Sorry about that.
AMY. There's a woodchuck. He's always . . . like comin' around.
TOM. No kiddin'. I guess you must be Amy, right?
AMY. Why? Who . . . ?
TOM. I'm Mr O'Toole. Friend of Angela? Remember Angela? She talked to you this morning on the phone. Said I was coming.

   AMY *simply waits expectantly.*

TOM. Could we go in and sit down for a minute? I'm not the police, I'm a private investigator. I'm looking into the Dr Daniels murder, you remember that? – Abe Daniels?

   She turns and walks up to the house, he following; she is escaping as unnoticeably as she can.

TOM (*walking behind her*). Angela says you were very helpful during the trial and I was wondering if I could talk about a few . . .

She opens a screendoor and a frightened chicken flies right out past her head, but she seems not to notice.

Interior: AMY's *house – Same time*

TOM *follows* AMY *into the living room, a mess: broken couch, a sleeping dog, and half a dozen chickens strolling about. She doesn't sit, but stands like one of the chickens, staring at nothing.*

TOM *reaches down into a bare clay pot and pulls out . . . an egg!*

AMY *glances at it.*

AMY. That's an egg.
TOM (*at least this is some progress*). Right!
AMY. Jerry doesn't live here any more.
TOM (*gently replacing the egg*). Which Jerry is that, dear?
AMY. The one who killed that Dr Daniels . . .

Straight-faced, TOM *lets a beat pass.*

TOM. I wonder if you could help me out, Amy. See I'm comin' in a little late and there's some things I'm not clear on . . . Like to sit down?

He draws a chair closer for her and she sits, looking at him with some surprise at his kindness.

You know, don't you, that there's a man in prison for killing Dr Daniels.
AMY. Oh no, he didn't do it, Jerry did it.
TOM. Gee whiz, that's what Angela's been tellin' me. But I'm glad to hear it from another person . . . Incidentally, how do you come to know Angela?

AMY. Angela? . . . Bimini.

TOM. Bimini . . . you mean down the Caribbean?

AMY's expression changes – she seems to relate momentarily.

AMY. I told all this to the cops, though . . . And then Jerry went down.

TOM. Jerry went where, dear?

AMY. To the cops. He was all covered with blood.

TOM. And what did the cops do?

AMY. They sent him here to go to sleep.

TOM. He told the cops he'd killed Dr Daniels?

AMY. He was going crazy about it, so I said you better get it off your mind 'cause he's so religious; he's raised Catholic, you know.

TOM. Where is Jerry now, dear, do you know?

AMY. He might be in the cemetery, but I don't think he's dead.

TOM. . . . Why do you think he's in the cemetery if he's not dead, dear?

Sleep threatens to overcome her then and there . . . she goes to the couch.

TOM. Amy?

AMY. Well, praying there to Major McCall.

TOM (*it is getting more and more weird*). Praying to Major McCall?

AMY. . . . Or to his church, maybe – you know, the mill.

TOM. And where would that be located, darlin'?

AMY. Like by the Winslow Bridge . . . or ah . . . Yeah, where you come down to the river . . . You know . . . that mill . . . (*She breathes deeply, falls fast asleep.*)

Exterior: Cemetery – Dusk

TOM *moves, glancing about at the grave-markers and monuments. His eye is caught by a base with the monument broken off and removed. He touches the broken cement which once joined the two. He reads the inscription. Close-up:*

> MAJOR JEROME SETH MCCALL
> POET AND SOLDIER
> HIS LIFE FOR THE NATION
> 1825 – 1862

Now he sees, on the ground at the foot of the monument's base, what look like burned bones in a little pile. The grass around the pile is blackened. He stands and walks toward his car nearby.

Exterior: TOM's *car – Day*

TOM *is on a road above the river when he sees a motorcycle approaching; the rider – this will turn out to be* JERRY *– has both arms raised in the air and is facing up to the sky as though imploring heaven.*

TOM *quickly pulls over to stick out his head, and watch the man who disappears around a turn. Then he drives on. In a moment he stops the car, seeing . . .*

Exterior: Abandoned mill – River – Day

It is a large New England mill, long since abandoned, beside the river. The Winslow Bridge, as AMY *had specified, is in the near distance.*

Exterior: Abandoned mill – Day

TOM *is approaching the mill fairly cautiously. Notes the broken window panes, the weeds around the front door. Opens it and walks in.*

Interior: Abandoned mill – Day

An immense space, a shambles of old broken machinery. The light from the windows is sepulchral; as TOM's *eyes adjust he sees an object standing against a wall, goes to it.*

The statue of a Civil War major, sword in scabbard, proudly moustached, one foot forward – the conventional Civil War monument. It has been placed on a rough base, a wooden box. A few candles stand before it.

He moves about and sees a rumpled cot, a dented kerosene stove with a pot on it and a few cans of beans nearby.

Now he sees a live lamb in a makeshift pen.

He walks to a wide loading door on the water side of the building, looks out on a boat-landing ramp or pier.

He turns now to return to the door through which he entered, and practically walks into ANGELA. *She is dressed now in a navy-blue straight-cut suit, carrying a rather sedate leather handbag.*

TOM. Jesus! – Boy, you scared me! Whatcha doin' here?

She stares at him, strangely, without immediately answering. Her eyes seem to see inward, rather than out. She seems somehow different than before – stands with a certain elegance, almost aloof, her vocal tone deeper in the throat and cultivated, although the grammar is not quite perfect.

ANGELA. Why didn't you tell me you were coming here?
TOM (*mystified, searching her odd look*). Well, Amy said he might be here . . .
ANGELA. 'What Amy said' is hardly consequential.
TOM (*absolutely baffled*). Hey, look, I'm only . . .
ANGELA (*with haughty command*). We're going to have to discuss this if you intend to continue.

Mystified, TOM *decides to let this pass for the moment, and points to the Major's statue and the penned lamb.*

TOM. What's this about, do you know?

ANGELA *glances down at the sacrifice; there is some loaded quality to her simple reply.*

ANGELA. It's his religion.
TOM. Jerry?

She looks up at the Civil War soldier's statue, and it seems to touch her with some reverential feeling . . . which she instantly dispels.

ANGELA (*factually*). He believes the Major is God and that he's His son.

As she says this TOM *detects the barest suggestion that she may share this belief, and is even feeling out his reaction.*

TOM. Well, he's got a right, I guess. – Is this a one-man religion or . . . ?
ANGELA. Oh, there was a group once, but . . . they're practically all gone off now. You know.
TOM (*a stab*). Were you in it?
ANGELA (*rather quickly*). No, but . . . (*She looks up at the Major. And now defensively . . .*) Our Father's house has many mansions, you know.

He doesn't reply, trying to fathom her, for she has a different tonality than earlier, a certain command.

But listen, I want you to tell me before you decide to take off after somebody again, you understand?
TOM. Hey, hold it now . . .
ANGELA. Well you want to know what's involved, don't you? – before you get hurt or something?
TOM. Kid, if I'm doing the investigation I make those decisions, not you.
ANGELA (*flaring up incredibly fast*). Don't you understand *anything*?

She hesitates a moment, then turns and starts away. He lunges out and stops her.

TOM (*friendly, but decisive*). You want to tell me what's going down here, Angela, or should I go home now and stay there?

ANGELA (*her brows knit*). Why are you calling me that kind of name?

TOM. What name you want me to call you?

ANGELA (*with a nuance of haughtiness*). Why Renata, of course.

She walks away. Dumbstruck, he stares after her.

Interior: TOM's *bathroom – Day*

He is drying off after a shower. Through the half-open door he sees CONNIE *entering the bedroom with fresh sheets. Wrapping the towel around him he goes halfway toward her.*

TOM. Incidentally, I've just about decided to cut out of that Abe Daniels case.

CONNIE. Boy, that's good news. I thought she sounded off the wall from day one.

TOM. Well, some of her information *has* checked out, but . . . she's just too complicated. It's like chasing feathers in a tornado. I'm telling her this morning. (*Pats her cheek gently.*) I feel better already.

Interior: Coffee shop – Next day

Close shot: A woman's beautiful legs folding one over the other. Pulling back, we see TOM *trying not to stare at the woman at a nearby table in a coffee shop where he sits at the counter having his cup. He pays and walks into the street.*

The madness of his awakened sexuality is bubbling in him and wherever he turns he can see only temptation. In the street, the shop windows, stepping down from a halted bus, getting into cars, their photos on magazines at the newsstand – the bodies of women assault him like a naked army.

Suddenly he sees her waiting for a light to change . . . ANGELA standing there, available, his own if he wants her. His brain shatters and as she steps off the curb to cross the avenue he rushes and calls after her . . .

TOM. Ang . . . (*Breaks off – remembering.*) Renata! Hey!

She doesn't turn around. Now he is a few feet behind her . . .

Renata?

She still doesn't turn around.

Angela?

Now she turns.

ANGELA (*immensely happy to see him*). Hello! Where you been, why haven't you rung me?

TOM. Listen, what am I supposed to call you – Renata or Angela?

ANGELA (*mystified*). Renata? What do you mean?

TOM. Well, the other day in that place by the river . . .

ANGELA. . . . Oh God. Did I do a number or something?

She breaks off, the blood draining out of her face, and he grips her arm.

Get me home, will you?

Alarmed, he helps her to walk.

Interior: TOM's *car – Day*

ANGELA *is deeply upset, staring ahead. The car is parked in a lot behind the courthouse.*

TOM. Listen . . . I was coming over to tell you that I'm pullin' out of the case.

She turns to him, incredulous, deeply shocked and lost. But his indecision begins returning as he realizes her need.

Let's face it, kid, I'm not getting the story from you.

ANGELA (*bravely, letting him feel her hurt, she gives him a wounded smile*). Okay, Tom. (*Gives his arm a pat.*) I know when I lose. But I'm not giving up on Felix. Can you get me home?

TOM (*takes her hand; his look has become desperate*). I don't think I want to lose you.

ANGELA (*a witty grin and toss of her head*). Then don't.

TOM (*delaying the end . . .*). Frankly, I've had the thought that . . . I'd really love to take a shot at shaking up the prosecutor.

ANGELA (*an electric reaction – excited but tinged with alarm*). Callaghan?

TOM (*sensing more than mere curiosity*). . . . You know him?

ANGELA (*evading, but expertly*). Well . . . you know, like everybody.

TOM. I'd love to put the fear of God in that college boy. Just to see what drops out. You never know, y'know?

ANGELA. Do I love brass balls!

She grasps his face and plants a deep kiss on his mouth.

TOM. I love you, Angela. (*Quickly grips his head.*) Now what the hell'd I say that for!

ANGELA (*moved*). Oh, you're dear! Let's go home!

TOM. Yes, mam!

He starts to drive. As she lifts an arm to straighten her hair he sees the edge of bandage around her wrist.

What's that?

ANGELA (*there is some conflict*). . . . I . . . had an accident yesterday.

TOM. When?

ANGELA (*she hesitates: he sees this: then she decides to let him know*). A guy came up behind me and threw me against a car.

TOM. What!! Why?

Their eyes meet.

ANGELA. A cop, I think. Out of uniform.

His face hardens in fury.

Interior: CALLAGHAN's *office – Next day*

TOM, BELLANCA, CALLAGHAN. BELLANCA, *Chief of Detectives, is in full stride. This is* JOHN CALLAGHAN's *courthouse office;* BELLANCA *is both subservient and contemptuous of his classy, alcoholic superior. Toward* TOM *he is openly sarcastic.*

BELLANCA. I mean, John, you can't seriously be asking us to listen to his crap! I know the woman he's been talking to – Angela Crispini, and she's as crazy as a worn-out whore can get!

TOM. Bellanca, I made up my mind at breakfast that I'm not gonna get mad all day . . .

BELLANCA. Oh, give us a break, O'Toole – who gives a shit if you get mad?

TOM (*turning to* CALLAGHAN). I came to tell you that I have been retained on the Epstein case, to find new evidence that will get him a retrial. I am asking for cooperation from the relevant personnel. I am not on a vendetta. I pounded a Chicago beat for a lotta years . . .

BELLANCA (*to* CALLAGHAN). Till they threw him out, I heard.

TOM (*still to* CALLAGHAN). There is no question in my mind that Felix Epstein is innocent and I want him out of jail.

BELLANCA. You finished?

TOM. Bellanca, you got the wrong man and the smart thing would be to face it now.

BELLANCA (*furious, he stands; to* CALLAGHAN). The woman who is feedin' him this garbage is an alcoholic and a hooker for twenty years! (*Counts on his fingers.*) The Ramada Inn, the Hilton, Looie's 48 Club, Ritchy's Truck Stop – you name it she's hooked there, and he's taking her word against ours! (*To* TOM.) Felix Epstein killed his uncle, period!

BELLANCA *shoulders his way to the door and goes out.* TOM *seems slightly shaken, but is still furious.*

CALLAGHAN (*barely concealing his gladdened heart*). Okay . . . this department will not obstruct any legitimate investigation of the Epstein case.

TOM. I will want to look at evidence.

CALLAGHAN. If we've got it you can see it.

TOM. Right.

He stands, goes to the door.

CALLAGHAN. O'Toole?

TOM *turns.*

You will never get Epstein – A. B: this is the biggest mistake of your life. See you around.

TOM, *filled with anger and uncertainty, leaves fast.*

Interior: ANGELA's *bedroom – Evening*

TOM *is just entering the room.* ANGELA *is sitting up in bed in a negligee, busily writing in a notepad. Beside her, a file folder lies open, filled with newsclips, jottings, etc . . .*

ANGELA. Be right with you. I know a wonderful pasta joint, you like ziti?

TOM. Couple of things we got to discuss, Angela, before we go out – I really have to.

ANGELA, *stuffing notebook in folder, gets off bed, crossing room.*

ANGELA. God, you're a great-looking man.

He watches her as she puts the folder into a file, which she shuts, snaps the large padlock, and closes the drape over it.

TOM (*intent on clarification*). Angela, I been going over in my mind . . .

ANGELA. You're my first since I gave up on it and I can't get it out of *my* mind.

TOM. Well, I can't tell you what it's meant to me.

ANGELA. Why not tell me? Please, Tom. (*She snuggles to him, anticipating.*) Let's just talk; not about the case . . . just anything. You reading anything lately? I'm just finishing the biography of Joan Crawford by her daughter. Did you read that?

TOM (*with a grin*). I'm not too big on trash.

ANGELA. Well some trash is interesting but I thought it was uncalled for . . . I mean, her own *daughter*. My father raped me, but I'm not writing books about him.

TOM. Really raped you?

ANGELA. For years. By the same token, though, with people like him it wasn't, you know, all that unusual with a daughter. But it sure did *me* in.

TOM *stares at her for a moment. Then remembers his point.*

TOM. This is important, kid, so let's . . .

ANGELA. It's not important a woman was raped?

TOM (*openly impatient*). Now listen, Angela, it's out in the open now that I'm on the case . . . I don't want to make a fool of myself – I have to know what your involvement is, okay?

He notes an inexplicable sort of tension coming over her, an internalized quality walled off from him.

ANGELA (*strained, highly anxious*). I told you. Abe Daniels was my *doctor* . . .

Her breathing is deeper, flooding with some anxiety, she is clenching and unclenching her hands.

TOM. And Felix? – you really never knew him before the trial?

ANGELA (*angrily offended*). I don't understand, you mean I can't be upset by an innocent man bein' put away?

TOM. Sure you can, but I am layin' my whole reputation on the line here! The least you can do is level with me . . . ! I mean . . . (*He breaks off, aware now of her transformation.*)

ANGELA (*she stands; voice like gravel, her whole aspect is transforming into a crude streetwalker*). Caman, will ya, why don't you just come out with it . . . !

TOM *looks up at her, startled.* ANGELA *is strangely freed, one hip thrown out, arms akimbo, mouth distorted into a tough sneer.*

What you really mean is where does a fuckin' whore come off trying to . . .

TOM. Now wait, I did not call you a . . . (*He catches himself.*)

ANGELA. Go on, you're full of shit – you know I been a hooker.

TOM. Angela, I –

ANGELA. Screw this 'Angela!' What's this 'Angela'? (*Cupping her breasts to thrust them forward, she mimics him.*) Grab onto this you jerked-off choirboy . . . come on, get your finger out of your yum-yum and try some of this!

TOM (*holding his head*). Holy God.

ANGELA. Go on, you don't kid me . . . (*She turns, trying to force his hand onto her buttocks.*) Grab hold, you fucking milk-face, you think you're better than anybody else?

TOM. Angela, Jesus . . . !

A struggle; he forces her onto the bed. She screams and tries to fight him off, loses her wind, gasping, as he stands up. Watching him . . . pushing his hand off.

ANGELA (*she is clearly transported to another time and place, and he is a total stranger to her*). Well, if you can't get it up get goin'. I've got a line into the street tonight. Tip the hat-check girl – if you can part with a dollar. And the name is Leontine in case you want to ask for me next time.

ANGELA *has gradually lost an inner pressure and seems to fall asleep.* TOM *goes and bends over her, moved and mystified. Draws a blanket over her. Then he straightens up and peers into the air and leaves the room.*

Interior. Living room – Same time

TOM *is undoing the locks of the living-room door when she calls from the bedroom.*

ANGELA (*awakening*). Tom?! . . . Tom, please don't leave! Let me explain . . . !

Slowly, TOM *walks back to the bedroom.*

Interior: Bedroom – Same time

ANGELA *is sitting on the bed.* TOM *seats himself in a chair facing her, waiting.*

ANGELA *in shame lowers her eyes contritely and speaks in a whisper. Her secret is out.*

ANGELA. I'm sorry, Tom, I should have leveled with you, but I wasn't sure you'd understand.

He waits.

(*Taking a breath.*) I'm a . . . I mean I have like schizo tendencies, Tom. I . . . like break up.

TOM. Are you under psychiatric care?

ANGELA. I used to be. Abe sent me to this Dr Levy. But I haven't had episodes in about three years. I'm just under a lot of stress right now, see. But it doesn't mean I don't tell you the truth, you understand?

TOM. It's just that the way you suddenly come at me just now. And over at Jerry's place.

ANGELA (*a clear flowering of anxious uncertainty*). Jerry's place?

TOM. You said your name was Renata. You don't remember that *at all*?

ANGELA. In a way, but it's . . . What else?

TOM. That I must never go tracking anybody without your permission . . .

ANGELA. Tracking who? Who was I talking about?

TOM *is amazed.*

TOM. This Jerry who everybody says killed Daniels.

ANGELA (*trying to penetrate the fog, alarmed*). *Jerry*?

TOM. We'll have to clarify this. I can't be asking anybody's permission to follow my leads.

ANGELA. But that's impossible!

TOM. It's the way it's gotta be.

ANGELA (*as certain as she is, it seems suddenly distant to her . . .*). But Jerry . . . died.

TOM. Died!

ANGELA (*grips her head for a moment, trying to clear her mind*). Couple of months ago . . . in Georgia, or Alabama someplace . . . Amy told me. He'd get loaded and ride his bike with his arms . . . (*She starts lifting her arms.*)

TOM (*flinging his arms into the air*). Up in the air.

ANGELA. How'd *you* know?

TOM. I saw him do it on the road near his church.

ANGELA. But it's impossible . . .

She presses her hands to her temples, alarm in her face. And now he is scared for his own sanity.

TOM. I saw a man on a bike doin' that! – Look, you could have misunderstood Amy; she's so drugged-up it's hard to make out what she's saying – or maybe he did get hurt down there and recovered now.

ANGELA *lies down on the bed, deeply worried and exhausted.*

You want to go to sleep?

ANGELA. Please sit here.

She pats the bed; he moves from the chair to sit beside her. An intimacy of tone now.

TOM. I don't mean to be leanin' on you, honey, but I'm goin' up against the whole power structure on this one and I hate to do that blind on one side . . .

ANGELA *is visibly filling with emotion as she looks at him; now lays a hand on his, she lifts it reverently to her mouth, kisses it, sets it back and chastely removes her hand from it. He smiles, embarrassed and moved. Now, after a clear hesitation, he takes her hand and kisses it. Tears burst into her eyes.*

ANGELA. Tom?

TOM (*he has crossed one bridge now*). Yes.

ANGELA. I used to be with Abe.

TOM. *Abe Daniels?* I thought he was such a pillar.

ANGELA *is staring straight up with this.*

ANGELA. Abe saved me. He paid for Dr Levy, my psychiatrist. I will always owe Abe. (*That was said like a vow, solemnly.*)

TOM (*deeply stirred*). He sounds great. Must've been some shock then, heh.

ANGELA. Butchered. And the killer practically advertising himself and they go and put Felix away . . . I can't stand it! . . . Listen, I want to talk to you for days, but I have to feel we're friends . . .

TOM. I've never known anybody it was so hard to get a fix on.

ANGELA (*feeling slightly released, smiling*). Well, I've got a lot of sides . . . But that makes it more interesting, doesn't it?

As though unable to hold back any longer, she suddenly comes up off her pillow and, grasping his face, kisses him on the mouth with a strangely determined desperation.

Oh, Tom, I need you . . . !

TOM. Honey, please . . . we've got to discuss the . . .

She unzips his sports shirt . . .

TOM (*laughing now as the whirlpool takes him down*). Hey . . . hey! Wait! Hey!

She lowers her open mouth onto his stomach and he laughs. She is mounting him like a rock in a torrent, triumphantly smiling down at him.

TOM. Oh, God, I'm flyin'!

ANGELA (*laughing in victory*). Fly, baby, fly!

Interior: Courthouse evidence-locker – Day

A nondescript storage room in the courthouse basement. TOM is at a table sorting through a box of Abe Daniels' effects – bloodied clothing, etc. Finds a manila envelope, opens it and removes several photos which he shuffles until, coming on one, he stares at it.

Close shot: Photo – Daniels' living room. Taken soon after the murder, it shows a blood-drenched carpet, blood over the wall behind it, furniture overturned, chaos. The photo becomes real.

Interior: Daniels' living room – Sometime later – Day

The room is now empty of furniture or carpet; sun is shining through barred windows. MRS HEARST, a real estate agent, is selling hard.

MRS HEARST. . . . And as you can see, it's a very well-protected house – the windows are barred on all floors, and you have a kennel out there for the dogs . . . (*She swings open the front door and points up at an overhead TV monitor.*) and this camera tells you who's at the door before you open it.

TOM (*indicates a built-in screen near door*). Terrific . . . we're nuts on security.

MRS HEARST. You have children, Mr Franklin?

TOM (*continually taking in the place*). Seven. But only four are still home.

MRS HEARST (*confidentially*). I think you could get a steal on this place . . . you know . . . after what happened . . .

TOM. I was thinkin' the same. (*He is examining the five locks on the front door.*) Five locks! Boy, he sure wasn't kiddin' about lockin' up . . .

MRS HEARST. I know the estate would consider any reasonable offer . . .

TOM (*one final look around*). Think they'd take a million?

MRS HEARST. Well . . . I could certainly enquire.

TOM. Please do. I've got to be running now . . . you have my card . . .

MRS HEARST (*reading from the card in her hand*). That's the Franklin Periscope Company?

TOM. Correct – we service all the submarines. Talk to you soon.

He walks out the front door.

Exterior: AMY's *house – Later*

TOM *is moseying around the shabby place, but moving in the direction of the front porch – his eyes are roving everywhere for anything significant. The front yard is a cycle-nut's mess, plus a rusting old car or two. He climbs up on the front porch, knocks on screen door; no response. Looks in window.*

TOM (*calling*). Amy? You home?

No reply. He comes down porch steps to return to his car, parked yards away, when he is startled by something inside one of the rusting car wrecks. He walks over.

AMY *is sitting on the broken back seat, which rests on the car's floor, dressed in jeans and a man's jacket, two or three illustrated magazines open around her. She has a bruised cheekbone. She is petting a hen on her lap.*

TOM. Hiya, Amy.

AMY (*as though his appearance were perfectly ordinary*). Oh, hi.

TOM. Watcha readin'?

AMY. About crocheting.

TOM (*enthusiastically*). No kiddin'! You do crocheting?

AMY (*warmed by his interest*). Maybe I'd take it up. 'Cause people would buy them.

TOM. Say, I'll bet! – Your friend Jerry wouldn't be around, would he? I'd like to meet him.

AMY. He died, you know.

TOM. So I hear. But he's back ain't he?

AMY. Yeah, he's over at Robie's . . . I'm wondering if I ate today.

TOM. . . . Tell ya . . . I was about to go get myself a big pizza; would you two like to join me?

AMY (*her tongue running over her lip*). I guess so; we could go over and get him.

TOM. That's just what I was thinkin'! – What happened to your eye?

AMY. Oh . . .

With a denigrating wave of her hand she hungrily starts for his car across the yard's debris, but he watches her with marked curiosity as they make their way . . .

Exterior: Car – Day

AMY *is just pointing out* ROBIE'S *to* TOM, *and he sees . . .*

Exterior: ROBIE'S *shop and abandoned mill – Day*

TOM'S *point of view. The two places are not far apart on the river.*

Exterior: ROBIE's *tractor shop – Day*

A chaotic scene; 'Robie's' sells new and used and unusable tractors which stand scattered across a large field in front of his steel shed. Intermixed are auto wrecks and motorcycle remains, alongside new tractors in crates.

The immense sliding doors of the shed are always open; amid the chaos inside are parts bins and a new tractor or two being assembled, or a snow plow or mower being set up for delivery to a customer. But not yet a sign of a human.

TOM *is moving amid the stuff looking around for somebody.* AMY, *meanwhile, has found a litter of kittens under a machine and is sprawled on the ground trying to entice them out so she can pet them.*

TOM *comes to what appears to be an eight-by-twelve office and looks in through the doorway, finding rotund, seventy-three-year-old* ROBIE *scraping bread dough into two trays before a filthy-looking oven. Beside the oven is a cot with a feather blanket in disarray and a not too clean pillow. Against the walls are file cabinets, a rolltop desk permanently decked with invoices and odd tractor parts and next to it an old refrigerator and stove with a stew cooking on it.*

As TOM *arrives in the doorway he sees* ROBIE *with a knife making a mark on the dough with a certain intensity, closing his eyes as though in prayer.*

Close shot: Bread and knife: The knife is making the mark of an inverted cross in the dough.

ROBIE *gingerly removes two finished loaves out of the oven – each similarly marked – and brushing away some urgent mail, he sets the loaves on his desk. Now he puts the two trays of fresh dough into the oven.*

TOM. Excuse me.

ROBIE, *snapping his finger against the crusts, he listens for the sound, paying no attention to* TOM.

TOM. That sure smells good.

ROBIE (*wryly – he has a pipe in his mouth*). Well, buy yourself a tractor and I might throw in a loaf.

TOM. Could I buy one of *them*?

ROBIE. Oh no. They're not for sale, they're just for – you know – just us.

TOM. – I'm lookin' for Jerry, wouldn't be around, would he?

ROBIE. They're all out there someplace. Sonny?

TOM *turns to face* SONNY, *who is bald, about six foot seven and keeps shifting his weight from one foot to the other and is carrying a large transmission main gear. He stammers.*

SONNY. Pa, do-do-do we get one of these o-o-off a John D-D-Deere 941?

ROBIE. You can't be carryin' that with your hernia.

SONNY. It's okay – I been prayin' over it. Don't hurt at all now.

ROBIE. We'll be prayin' over you if you keep liftin'. (*Taking the gear from him.*) He's looking for Jerry.

SONNY. Sure, here's Jerry.

TOM *follows* SONNY *into the tangle of machinery, tractors up on blocks, rubbish . . .* SONNY *stops, once surrounded with machines, takes a folded-up magazine out of his hip pocket, and with a shy smile . . .*

Would you like to re-re-read so-so-something in-in-interesting about G-God?

TOM *takes the magazine, unfolds it. 'SATAN'S WORD' in large letters decorates the cover over the same sign of the inverted cross as was cut into the bread.*

SONNY (*voice over*). It'll d-d-do you a lot of g-g-good.

KENNY MONTANA *appears, a fierce-looking monster, maybe three hundred pounds, a heavy breather with a black fedora, black moustache, and the look of a Sumo wrestler. He doesn't speak often, but stares a lot instead, and without expression.*

He appears from around a machine so that TOM *suddenly finds himself face-to-face with him and his cryptic silence.* SONNY *moves off and* TOM *gladly follows him, with* MONTANA *bringing up the rear, breathing.*

They discover JERRY; *he is in a corner of the shop working on his motorcycle. Like the other two men he has a forest simplicity in his gaze. He also has a ten-inch hunting knife sticking up out of his riding boot and is a long-time addict of most of the known drugs but is for the moment clear-eyed, with a searching look and a certain mystifying depth.*

SONNY, *by far the most sociable of the three, shifting from foot to foot, gestures awkwardly toward* JERRY.

TOM. Hiya, I'm Tom O'Toole, friend of Angela? Angela Crispini?

JERRY *has turned from his bike but with only the mildest curiosity . . . or is it suspicion? The moment is saved by the arrival of* AMY *who is cradling two kittens in her arms, followed by the mother cat.*

AMY. I'm hungry.

As TOM *speaks now,* JERRY *stares quizzically into his eyes as though sensing some vaguely palpable center of gravity there . . . (every happening* means *something, if only one knew).*

TOM (*taking the plunge*). Glad a meet you, Jerry . . . Tell ya, I happen to be in the cemetery the other day and I seen those burned bones layin' there; I'm very interested in that – is that a sacrifice or . . . Watch it!!

The mother cat has dislodged a truck driveshaft which was leaning against the wall behind JERRY. *This six-foot tube of heavy steel begins toppling onto him.* TOM, *with an automatic reaction, violently pushes* JERRY *out of its way as it bounces on the cement floor with a resonating clang.*

In the excitement AMY *dropped the kittens, and now the cat is carrying one of them away in her mouth.*

For a moment AMY, SONNY, MONTANA *and* JERRY *stare at the cat moving away – they seem to feel some meaning in its action. Now* JERRY *turns to* TOM *as though seeing him in an aura. But his intensity could be hostility . . .*

TOM. . . . Sorry to push you, but . . .

JERRY (*a knowing, excited little grin*). You *felt* that comin', didn't you.

TOM. Well no, I saw the cat rub on it . . .

MONTANA. You the cops?

JERRY. No, he's famous. I seen you once on the TV.

TOM. Right. I'm tryin' to help Angela, kind of, you know?

JERRY, *as susceptible as anyone else to notoriety, turns and walks out into the field and halts, looking up at the sky.* SONNY *and* MONTANA *remain behind in the shop staring off at unpredictable* JERRY *with some expectancy.*

AMY (*calling to* JERRY *a bit more desperately*). He wants to buy a pizza! Okay?

TOM *goes out into the field to* JERRY. *His instinct is not to speak yet, but physically to communicate with him and hopefully to draw him out that way.*

JERRY *sits now on a piece of machinery in the field; the long knife in his boot is prominent.*

JERRY. Trouble with Angela is she can't communicate.

AMY *enters the shot, sits on the grass with the one of the kittens.*

She can't unload.

TOM (*as naively as he is able*). You think that's what she wants to do?

JERRY. It's what everybody wants to do – tell it, get rid of it, put it behind you. The Major could help but she won't let him.

SONNY *and* MONTANA *move into the shot, their arrival creates the feeling of a séance as they intently listen.*

AMY. He was almost a priest.

TOM (*alerted*). Say that's right; you're Catholic, aren't you?

JERRY. I wasn't normal enough for the priesthood – kept tryin' to get out over the wall to find girls. But I saw Jesus once. But he never come back. But the Major's *there*, man, he's *there*. But Angela's got nobody. So she keeps goin' off that way.

AMY. Can't we eat?

TOM. Goin' off how, Jerry?

JERRY. – Changin' herself into this one and that one. You've seen her do that, haven't you? But that's nothin' but psychic possession, that's never going to get her clear.

TOM. Clear of what, Jerry? I'm really trying to help her, see – what do you think is grabbing her?

JERRY (*stares into* TOM's *eyes a long moment*). You been to seminary, haven't you.

TOM. Funny you ask that – No. But I've got two brothers in the church, and my sister's a nun.

JERRY. I knew it. (*Shakes his head in wonder – a glimmer of warmth now.*) Can always tell.

His perceptiveness shown, he gets up, walks a couple of yards; TOM *follows, but when* SONNY *and* MONTANA *start to follow,* JERRY *turns to them sharply, but as much plea as command . . .*

I'm *talkin'* to this man!

They halt obediently. JERRY *turns his back on them, sits on one heel and slips the knife out of his boot.* TOM *kneebends to be on his level.*

Major give me this. People don't believe it, but he did. Read that?

TOM (*reads inscription on knife*). 'Grand Army of the Republic.' Huh! And he give you this?

JERRY. It was his battle knife from the Civil War. One night I come and it was layin' there right at his feet on top of his grave, shining in the moonlight. You believe it?

TOM. Why not?

AMY *moves into the shot.* JERRY *never takes his fascinated eyes from* TOM.

AMY. Don't I ever get to eat today! I'm hungry!

TOM. Come on, what you say? It's my treat.

JERRY. I'd like to talk to you . . . I never met one before.

TOM. One what?

JERRY. Meet you at the diner.

JERRY *walks away,* AMY *trailing behind, and* TOM *starts toward his car, excitement in his eyes.*

Interior: Diner – Later

TOM, AMY, JERRY. AMY *is gorging the last of a large pizza.*

JERRY (*gently stroking her hand, straightening her hair*). She backfired once and never been the same. I'm trying to straighten myself out, see, but I'm . . . I'm kind of loaded up all the time . . .

TOM. I'm reading you, Jerry . . .

JERRY. I know. I knew it soon as you looked at me. But it's . . . (*Sighs, shaking his head . . .*) so hard.

TOM (*lets a moment pass*). I know; but that shows you're not an animal, doesn't it – I mean there's lots that wouldn't be bothered at all.

This stab leaves JERRY *staring ahead. After a moment . . .*

JERRY. I think sometimes I died and came back, but I didn't . . . like get here yet.
TOM. I know the feeling. Some things can pull you down and under if you don't unload.
JERRY. I can't hardly breathe sometimes.
AMY. . . . There's somebody else involved, see.
TOM. Well . . . that makes it tougher.

TOM *watches* JERRY's *reaction to this revelation; but he calmly stands, lifts* AMY *to her feet with a magisterial touch.* TOM *hurriedly writes on a napkin, his excitement difficult to hold down. He stuffs the napkin into* JERRY's *shirt pocket.*

That's my home and office number . . . day or night, you hear? I'll be by again in a day or two, okay?

JERRY *looks up at him helplessly.* AMY *chews deliciously.* TOM *stands, tucking a bill under the ketchup bottle.*

Guess I don't have to tell you, Jerry – there's no power in the world strong enough to break a man's grip on his own throat.

JERRY *looks at him with recognition.*

But you know who *can*, don't you.

JERRY *stares ahead at the challenge.*

See ya.

Interior: DR LEVY's *office – Day*

LEVY, *fortyish, hip, sits behind his desk facing* TOM *who is seated with his coat in his lap.*

LEVY. . . . No-no, not schizophrenia – Mrs Crispini has a multiple personality. That's quite different.

TOM. I can't thank you enough for seeing me, Doctor – I'll be very quick. The big question for me is whether to believe her. I mean, coming on like that with these different personalities . . .

LEVY. A fear reaction – when she's frightened enough she changes her identity. It's something we all do but not to such an extreme degree.

TOM. In other words, I've got to look at her more as . . . really normal.

LEVY. Was there something specific?

TOM. You knew Dr Abe Daniels, I understand.

LEVY. Many years. Wonderful human being.

TOM. She claims to have been Dr Daniels' girl, and for a long time – is that credible to you?

LEVY (*he seems uncomfortable, almost apprehensive*). Well . . .

TOM. . . . Unless that gets into your medical relationship – I know she used to be your patient couple of years ago.

LEVY. I really shouldn't say any more. (*A glance at his watch.*) Afraid I'm out of time . . .

Stands – TOM *does too.*

I can understand your dilemma; she can be very contradictory . . .

Going to the door together . . .

TOM. Doctor, every time we talk I end up one foot's wet and the other one's dry! (*Laughs; they find themselves face-to-face, nodding in agreement . . .*) . . . That woman's a real piece of work, you know? I means she's an *original*!

They are chuckling into each other's face; it is a sudden, unforeseen communion, in effect they are celebrating her somehow . . . (and as this happens TOM *knows that* LEVY *has been her lover). A shy softness descends on* LEVY's *face as he speaks.*

LEVY. Mrs Crispini is one of those great levelers – the kind of woman who can put the peasant and the king on exactly the same level.

TOM. Right!

LEVY continues, but now a certain unresolved confusion of his own is entering into him.

LEVY. They can distort a man's vision . . . they can blind you, destroy your basic common sense . . .

They exchange a shared enthralled look – only for an instant, but it is enough for TOM to sense LEVY's connection to ANGELA.

TOM (*his gaze has a knowingness now*). Gotcha . . . Thanks again, Doctor. This's been very helpful.

Exterior: LEVY's street – Day

TOM is starting to drive away from LEVY's office – which is actually in a large Victorian house on a quiet residential street. Suddenly he notices ANGELA who is emerging from a cab in front of the house. He sees her go in. A look of quandary suffuses his face.

Exterior: Day

Skeet discs are being shattered against the sky with blasts of a shotgun. Backing, we find the shooter to be retired judge HARRY MARKS, a man in his late sixties. Former criminal lawyer, he has now turned rosy and wise, chews an unlighted cigar; lot of vanity here but also sentiment, when affordable.

Behind him is his great house, lawns, and TOM standing to one side admiring his accuracy. MARKS finishes the load, offers the gun to TOM.

MARKS. Want to try it?

TOM. Why embarrass myself? –

They walk toward the house.

Listen, Judge, don't be shy about throwin' me out if I'm taking too much time . . .

MARKS. Cut it out, Tom – I owe you my son's life; for you I have time. What's it about, this Crispini woman again?

TOM. I wanted to run some more stuff past you.

MARKS. Baby, I'm wondering if the time has come to ask you the obligatory question.

TOM (*embarrased*). Well . . . the answer is yes – But it's nothing – you know – serious.

They enter the house.

Interior: JUDGE MARKS' *study – Day*

MARKS *sits before a desk, on which are photos of himself with Ed Sullivan, Eisenhower, Stevenson, Reagan, etc . . .*

MARKS. For a romantic like you all sex is serious. Watch out! Just because you're screwing don't start believing everything she tells you.

TOM. Oh, no, I'm not . . .

MARKS. Strong sex always ends up the captain of the ship, and this captain sounds crazy to me. Now let's talk practical. I would think twice before going ahead with this case.

TOM. You serious?

MARKS. . . . This is our third discussion, Tom, and I still don't know why she got so interested in saving this Epstein fellow –

TOM (*abashed*). Look, that's all I've been trying to get out of her, but she . . .

MARKS. Tom, if she won't come clean you have got to get up and walk. This is basic.

TOM (*holding his head*). Harry, you're killing me . . . !

MARKS. All this time and you have nothing tangible about her connection! You're walking on bubbles!

TOM. Yes. I'm ashamed of myself – I guess I've been letting my dingus do my thinking. – Judge, I can't thank you enough. This is why I love to run things past you, you cut right to the gut of it.

MARKS. Callaghan'll eat you alive if you don't button this down tight . . . and I mean *tight*!

TOM. I'm absolutely clear now – she comes clean or I'm out. I can't thank you enough.

He starts to leave.

MARKS. Incidentally . . . I've read the transcript of Epstein's trial. She's quite right to be upset – All they proved in court was that he was in the doctor's house, but not that he killed anybody.

TOM (*his fears gone, depression over, he is almost shouting with revived indignation*). See? – this is what I mean! Callaghan did it again!

MARKS. But you've got to nail that woman! *Evidence*, not bubbles! – *where is she coming from*!

TOM. Right!! (*Pointing at* MARKS.) Bless every breath you take, Judge.

He stomps out full of juice.

Interior: TOM's *bedroom – Night*

CONNIE *is sleeping on her back;* TOM, *on his side, facing away from her. Her eyes open; she is mourning her life. He stirs.* CONNIE *half turns to him. He turns onto his back and they are staring at one another. His hand appears and cups her face. She is surprised, hardly dares smile; he raises up and kisses her. An awareness of his potency creeps into her eyes. He slides onto her and she almost laughs with astonished pleasure. He starts making*

*love and they are both experiencing renewed hope for themselves.
As climax approaches . . .*

The phone rings . . . CONNIE *pulls* TOM *into her even deeper.*

The phone rings again . . .

CONNIE *holds him tighter – willing them to an orgasm.*

The phone rings again . . .

ANGELA *will not give up –*

and neither will CONNIE.

Interior: TOM's *kitchen – Early morning*

In pyjamas and robe, TOM *is staring out at the first morning light
in the sky. His face is filled with bewilderment, but he has been
quickened, trying to figure himself out.* CONNIE *appears in frame
beside him, in a trim suit, dressed for school, reading her watch,
picking up her briefcase . . .*

CONNIE. Sorry I have to run; why don't you make yourself an
omelette?

TOM. Not hungry. (*Kisses her.*) Bye.

CONNIE. . . . Can't you smile? You're really very different
since you got on this case.

TOM (*he glances up at her with a troubled, slightly shamed smile*).
Well I'm frustrated. But the psychiatrist says she could be
tellin' the truth. And he used to treat her.

CONNIE. But how do you know she's not makin' it with him?

TOM (*astounded, gulping*). Now where do you come up with
an idea like that?

CONNIE. Why not? From the way it sounds, it's her way of
sayin' hello.

TOM. I can't stop now! – This Jerry character practically
confessed to me . . .

CONNIE. But he's an addict and he's crazy!

TOM (*menaced, he flies up*). I tell you there's something here
and she knows what it is. – And just incidentally, there's
still an innocent man in jail!

CONNIE. There always is.

TOM. Well there is, goddammit! – whether she's crazy or not!

Interior: Spaghetti joint – Day

TOM *and* ANGELA *are finishing dishes of spaghetti. She eats
sensuously. He watches her intently, but covers up with a good
imitation of ease.*

TOM. You eat everything like it's ice cream.

ANGELA (*indicating his half-full dish*). Aren't you going to
have it?

TOM. Not hungry.

She takes his dish and digs in.

ANGELA. Eating spaghetti is the second best thing in life.
(*Grinning.*) You still don't trust me, do you.

TOM (*trying to laugh*). For God's sake, Angela, I've laid my
whole professional life in your hands, and now I don't
trust you?

ANGELA. I don't understand it, there's something
changed . . .

TOM. All right, I'm going to admit something – I been to see
this Dr Levy, the psychiatrist you used to go to?

ANGELA (*cryptically*). What for?

TOM. Well, to be honest, I wanted his opinion about how . . .
how much to believe . . . of what you been telling me.

ANGELA (*on the verge of high resentment*). You don't say! And
what's his opinion?

TOM. He thinks you're absolutely believable.

ANGELA (*sunrise in her face*). Really! – How is old Levy? I
should go see him again, I haven't been there in so
long . . .

TOM (*eyes flattening at this lie*). Angela, listen . . . I happen to have seen you going into his office yesterday. I mean I have to say it.

She stands, gathers up her purse and coat, and starts to leave.

Now wait a minute! Angela! I didn't mean . . .

ANGELA (*furious*). I had to tell him! I didn't see any reason to mention it to you, but I had to!

TOM. Tell him what?

ANGELA (*tears forming*). About us. You've changed my life, Tom – I hadn't had anybody in nearly six months. I just had to tell somebody, it made me so happy.

Weeping she races into the street. TOM *follows.*

Exterior: Street – Same time

ANGELA *hurries down the street and stops suddenly.*

ANGELA. There's got to be trust!

TOM. Angela, listen to me . . .

ANGELA (*tough again*). . . . And anyway, O'Toole, without me, you're nowhere on this case.

TOM. I didn't say . . .

ANGELA. I haven't even begun; Jerry and Amy are nobody compared to who I could . . . (*Turning on him.*) Look if you don't want to go on okay, but there's an innocent man in jail! . . . or did I make that up, too?

TOM *stands there – conflicting emotions pulling at him.*

Interior: ANGELA'*s bedroom – Night*

They are in bed.

ANGELA. You like me a little?

TOM. A little?

Rolls onto his back, a depth of feeling in his eyes.

This is the most unexpected thing ever happened to me.

She watches him – a mixture of happiness with apprehension.

Can't you still trust me? Can't you tell me the story? I'm at the end of my rope, kid, I really am.

A last hesitation, and then . . .

ANGELA. Jerry was a runner. He ran drugs for Abe.

TOM. Dr Abe Daniels was in *drugs*?

ANGELA. He was the main man between here and Boston.

TOM. . . . Boy, I'm really out of it – that never crossed my mind. – But why didn't they arrest Jerry with all that blood on him?

ANGELA. He knows all the connections, and he's crazy enough to start talking.

TOM. Connections to . . . ?

ANGELA. Drugs and the police, the Detective Squad, Bellanca . . . Jerry's a timebomb on a motorcycle.

TOM. How come they didn't just waste him?

ANGELA. Maybe they will.

TOM. You mean if he keeps talking to me.

ANGELA (*nods*). And . . . those bulls working over in the shop with him. They're all disciples, you know.

TOM. Why'd Jerry do it to Daniels, Angela?

ANGELA (*shaking her head with remorse*). Oh, he'd built up this crazy idea – he really believed it – that Daniels had promised to build him a church for his new religion. And when he refused he went berserk. He'll do anything, you know.

TOM. And Callaghan was onto all this when he prosecuted Felix?

She barely nods, openly afraid.

He turned it all into a family fight between relatives.

She confirms with a glance.

Well . . . it all suddenly makes sense. And I can see why you always seem so terrified. – You are, aren't you.

Her helplessness moves him. He turns and glances over at a table on which several framed pictures stand. Picks up one of them, looks at it.

Close shot: ANGELA *on motor boat: She is in a bikini – a gangster type in sunglasses behind her – posing spread out on an open deck.*

TOM. Is this Bimini?

ANGELA *nods, her eyes full of calculations.*

Amy says now and then she and you would donkey the stuff up from there.

ANGELA. I stopped two years ago. I just couldn't stand the tension any more.

She genuinely weeps for a ruined life. He holds her close.

TOM. The cops must know about that, don't they?

She nods.

So how do you come to be beatin' on them with this case now?

His logic makes her turn her face to him – an imminent outrage in her eyes.

I have to ask, kid, I'm going up against some heavy hitters and I don't dig this!

ANGELA. Because I know how innocent Felix is and I can't bear it!

Open disbelief descends on his face and he makes no attempt to conceal it.

TOM. I gotta be gettin' home.
ANGELA. I have to tell you something.

He slips out of bed and begins to dress, and his failure to get excited by some new revelation enrages and alarms her.

I am trying to tell you something!

Resolutely deadpan, he simply sits on a chair facing the bed, leaving a space between them.

I used to be with John Callaghan.

TOM (*this seems total madness*). We're talkin' about the prosecutor now.

She barely nods; it is a confession with suffering attached. — He is straightfaced, but doubt is in his tone.

You were banging the prosecutor?

ANGELA. He set up an apartment over at Wyndham Place. He nearly left his wife.

TOM (*is this possible or complete insanity?*). No kiddin'.

ANGELA. The best two years of my life. Until he began rigging the case against Felix – then I just couldn't stand it any more.

She notes his less than utter rapture at this news.

But he suffered torments over having to do this – he goes to retreats, you know, in a monastery.

TOM. I must have missed his spiritual side – why'd he have to do it?

ANGELA. A man as important as Abe Daniels chopped up like that . . . they had to nail it to somebody, and Jerry was absolutely out – Jerry could bomb the whole police department plus both parties in this town in the bargain. This case goes to the top of the mountain, Tom, the *top*. That's why I'm scared.

She gets up, moves now with a verve and energy, acting out the story. TOM *watches mesmerized, trying to pierce the truth of*

*this outrageous, yet somehow circumstantially, convincing
story.*

We'd go out to John's place on the beach and sit staring at
the fire . . . tears were pouring down his cheeks, it was
killing him. I pleaded with him, 'You could end up
President of the United States,' I said, 'you could be
anything, but you cannot do this to an innocent man!' . . .
But Bellanca handed him the proof against Felix – that
stupid comb, and the jury believed it. And it was all lies.

A beat.

TOM. I'm going to ask you a question, Angela. It's very
important.

Intensification of alertness shows in her eyes.

How well have you known Jerry?
ANGELA. Pretty well.

*He gets the message which, again, has a double edge, hurting
him and offering the possibility of hard information.*

TOM. I got a gut feeling he'd like to confess to me. Would you
help me with him? He seems to still like you.

*She seems to struggle a bit with her breathing, in a high conflict
which she strives to conceal.*

ANGELA. Why would he confess?
TOM. I guess the same reason he ran to the cops after he killed
Daniels – he's afraid of God. – I don't want to scare him off
with a wrong move, so I thought the three of us might sit
down; him, you and I . . .
ANGELA (*at this, her vocal register thins, rising higher*). You'd
better be very careful with Jerry . . .

*She begins moving about. She is nearly struggling to breathe.
Can she fear* JERRY's *confessing?*

He can be very tricky, you know . . .

TOM. Oh, I know . . .

ANGELA. Don't say you know, you don't know!

Her swift slash of anger astonishes him. She is beginning to gasp now.

TOM. Okay. But if we could get him to unload in front of a lawyer, we've nailed the case . . .

ANGELA (*a deepening heaving of breath begins*). Yeah, but I can't imagine him . . .

TOM. But it's worth a big try, Ange, it's the whole ballgame, and I really think you owe it to . . . What's the matter?

She is nearly gasping for breath, and it stops him – she starts to lie down weakly on the bed, curling up in a defensive fetal position, and he starts to touch her hand . . .

Angela?

With a child-like cry she throws off his hand and quickly scampers into a corner, whimpering, hands raised protectively before her face. He is afraid to move and frighten her further . . .

ANGELA (*truly, a child's voice*). Please don't! Don't! Angie be good now!

TOM (*flabbergasted . . .*). Okay. Can I help you to bed?

Still whimpering, she allows him to approach and to pick her up in his arms, but suspicion is still at the edges of her eyes. He lays her down on the bed and she quickly looks sleepy, and curls up again.

All right, Angie . . . you try to sleep now, heh? – like a good little girl?

Her eyes flutter and close. He covers her with a blanket.

Stalemated, he stands thinking for a moment. He picks a polaroid photo of her off the table, and pockets it. Now her photo on the boat in Bimini catches his eye and he picks it up to study the gangster in it, blocking off her face with his hand. A sliver of paper sticking out under the photo's edge interests him; he draws out from behind the photo a newspaper photo of a man – JOHN CALLAGAHAN. *Glancing at her on the bed, he slips it into his pocket and leaves.*

Interior: Apartment-house lobby – Next day

It is a fairly posh lobby. TOM *enters from the street to face the uniformed* LOBBY-MAN.

TOM. Super around?

LOBBY-MAN. That door there. But there's no vacancies.

TOM (*taking bill out of his wallet*). Say, maybe you could help me, I'm trying to check something for Aetna Insurance, you ever see this woman?

He slips the bill to the man as he holds ANGELA's *polaroid photo up to him.*

LOBBY-MAN (*a puzzled look at the photo . . . then . . .*). Oh . . . sure, that's Mrs Crispini – Angela. Couple years ago, Apartment 6C.

TOM. Jeeze, thanks a whole lot. Tell me – she live there alone, or what?

LOBBY-MAN (*careful now . . .*). Well . . . you know . . .

TOM (*producing the newspaper photo of* CALLAGHAN *from a pocket . . .*). This man ever come by?

LOBBY-MAN (*studies photo; uncertain*). Well . . . (*Decides:*) No. (*But on the other hand . . .*) Wait a minute. (*Studies it again; shakes his head.*) I really don't know. Maybe. – Lot of people coming in and out of here . . .

TOM (*nods, stashes both photos*). Thanks. Take care of yourself.

He hurries out to the street, elated – ANGELA *is legit!*

Interior: Church – Day

TOM *is seated midway back in the nearly empty church, observing as, at the altar,* FATHER MANCINI *is giving* ANGELA *the wafer and blessing. (A previous communicant is just departing.)*

The intense, silent exchange of intimate feeling between her and the fascinated young priest, as she opens her mouth with uplifted eyes locked on his gaze, are a shock to TOM. *And as she approaches him now there is a mixture of amazement and disgust on his face.*

Cut to:

Interior: Vestry room – Day

TOM, MANCINI. *Throughout this scene* TOM *is intrigued by the idea that she has seduced this priest. They are entering the room . . .*

MANCINI (*putting away his vestments*). Thank you so much for coming today. Angela's spoken so often about you that I thought we should meet.

TOM. She's talked about you, too, Father – I think you're her favorite fella in the whole world right now.

MANCINI. Not quite – I think you are.

With a professional chuckle he sits on a window seat, thinking out his next words; he has a naive, sensuous face, rampant with idealism.

She's terribly worried, you know, that you may break off your commitment to the Epstein case.

TOM. Father, a lot depends on whether she can get herself to tell me where she's comin' from; why is she in this case, do you know?

MANCINI (*surprised*). But it's obvious – she is a profoundly idealistic woman!

TOM. But Father, why is it like pulling teeth to get the simplest facts out of her? She's driving me crazy with this cat-and-mouse . . .

MANCINI. Mr O'Toole, please – let me say only one thing to you – You are her lifeline now.

TOM is flattered, but baffled by this.

I'm not sure you realize that . . .

Camera emphasizes his spiritual sensuality here – perhaps stained glass rises behind him and he stands in a halo of light and his transfixed eyes almost convince TOM of the incredible fact behind his emotion . . .

She is a woman who has sinned; but somehow she challenges us – you must have felt that challenge, haven't you? – the challenge to live life, to care, to live up to our claims to responsibility and love of humanity; for her, to think is not sufficient – we must act, we must perform deeds in the world . . . ! This woman is the very spirit of *love*!

During this speech, intercut TOM's face, with his shocked realization that MANCINI is probably her lover. Moreover, he is saying what TOM himself has been feeling about ANGELA.

In MANCINI's mid-flight, slowly fade to:

Interior: TOM's car – Sundown

TOM is just pulling up in front of ANGELA's house.

ANGELA (*starting to open the car door*). Comin' up, aren't you?

TOM. Close the door a second.

She does. He lays a paternal hand on hers. His inner exhaustion is beginning to show.

I got a call this morning from one of the guards at the Penitentiary, a friend of mine. About Felix. Seems he is going through the bottom . . . he's suicidal.

ANGELA. But I just wrote him again . . .

TOM (*delicately*). The thing is, honey . . . I love bein' with you, but I – I think I better be spending my nights running down whatever I can find.

ANGELA *is hurt and apparently angry.*

ANGELA. Okay.

TOM. Well, you understand why I'm saying this, don't you?

ANGELA (*archly*). Y'know, incidentally, I went to Mary Immaculate High School which just happens to be the highest-rated school in the state . . .

TOM (*to head off an explosion*). Oh, now look . . .

ANGELA. Because sometimes you talk to me like my head's full of gravel. – Listen, you cutting out?

TOM. Angela . . .

ANGELA. Then cut! It's the story of my life!

She pulls her door open and is getting out.

TOM (*angered*). Dammit, I didn't mean it that way . . . !

She being out of his reach, he opens his door and starts to get out.

Exterior: Street – Same time

TOM *has practically emerged into the side of a squad car, which has glided to a halt next to his, and he is looking into the face of* BELLANCA, *in the passenger seat beside a cop driver.*

BELLANCA *wears a supercilious grin, glances similarly to* ANGELA, *then signals to the cop driver and rides off down the street. When* TOM *turns back to* ANGELA . . .

Close-up: ANGELA. *She is suppressing great, trembling fear, staring down the street at the departing detective.*

TOM *enters shot. She looks up at him and swallows. Without waiting for him she hurries up her stoop, and he follows.*

Interior: ANGELA's *apartment – Moments later*

They are just entering. She turns the three locks on the door, fixes the chain in place and hurries through the unused living room to the bedroom. TOM *follows.*

Interior: Bedroom – Same time

In silence, she gets out of her coat, hangs it in closet, finally sits on bed and stares. TOM, *still in coat and hat, sits, waiting for her to speak.*

ANGELA. Bellanca was following us.

TOM. I don't know – maybe he just happened to come by.

She looks at him with a certain mystified suspicion.

Just trying to keep it real, kid. (*He breaks off, to avoid alienating her.*)

ANGELA (*a plea, as well as fear – anger*). They've got a squad car parked on each corner some nights!

TOM. I never saw one, but I . . . (*Skeptically, tired of pretending.*) I wouldn't put it past them.

ANGELA (*weak with fear, she lies back*). Come over here.

He comes and sits on the bed beside her and she takes his hand.

On the street today . . . it's practically every time I go out now . . . right on Crowley Square, they pull up beside me and ride along slowly while I'm walking.

TOM. Why?

She suddenly pulls him down to her.

ANGELA. Hold me.

He wraps her in his arms, only half-willingly, still in his coat.

TOM. Angela . . . darlin'! Why don't you let me help you!

ANGELA. Oh, God, I worship you!

Weeping, she buries her face in him; his frustration mounts. Now she lies on her back, staring up.

They're trying to scare you away.

TOM (*separating from her*). That's good, I like makin' them nervous – Now look dear . . .

He sets himself for some difficult news, as she lies there looking up at him with her clear need. He holds out a hand to her, palm down, smiling – she senses a farewell and shows surprise . . .

I am not going to let Felix burn out up there, honey. (*Pause.*) Be well.

He moves to the door.

ANGELA. I have letters . . . from him.

He turns back to her at the door.

TOM. Who's that, dear?

ANGELA (*calming now, the struggle past*). John.

TOM. Callaghan?

She nods. A little tension laugh escapes him.

Like . . . what do you mean? Love letters or something?

ANGELA (*nods. Then . . .*). And about the case . . . One of them.

TOM (*still with a shred of skepticism*). Actually . . . referring to it?

ANGELA (*a longish pause*). Yes.

TOM. My God, Angela . . .

ANGELA. . . . . Asking me not to let the case get between us. Because of what he had to do.

He looks past her face to the padlocked cabinet.

TOM. If you got something like that – you know that wraps it all up, don't you?

ANGELA. I can't bear to do that to him, it would destroy him . . .

TOM. He is the chief law enforcement officer of this county and he knowingly rigs a murder case? He's *gotta* be destroyed.

ANGELA. I can't do that! . . . He's the love of my life.

TOM *stares at her.*

TOM. What the hell is going down here, are you using *me* or something? What've I been doing, standing in for John Callaghan? Answer me, dammit!

ANGELA. No, I'm through pleading for . . . for some respect, for Christ's sake!

TOM. *You* pleading! You pleading! I been on my knees since I walked into this! But listen . . . you got something to tell me, give me a ring. I'm hittin' the pike.

He resolutely starts out. She is trying to restrain herself, then can't any more . . .

ANGELA. When you get downstairs, see if there isn't a squad car parked on both corners of this block!

TOM. What squad cars, what are you talking about?

ANGELA. I wrote John last week that I would call you off the case if he would reinvestigate it himself. Next thing I know, there's two cars parked almost every night, one on each corner. Just sitting there.

TOM. And he's still the love of your life?

The contradiction sends her jumping angrily off the bed and she picks up a shoe and throws it.

ANGELA. All right, just get out. Get out!!

TOM. In other words – is this it? – you wanted me to investigate just enough to get Felix out – but not enough to implicate anybody you don't want to hurt. Is that the story? In other words, you are trying to get me to protect the bastards who put him in there! Well no wonder you're nervous –

He pushes both his arms back and forth in opposite directions. She is bending over, rocking in frustration.

You been trying to go north and south and powder your nose all at the time time! (*Laughing viciously.*) Well it can't be done, baby – not with me!

As he turns to go she straightens up from her crouch and with a cry from her belly . . .

ANGELA. HELP ME!

TOM. You read me one sentence in a letter from Callaghan – or even just show me his signature on one, okay? Do that, and I'm your man. Otherwise, *I am out!*

Clutching her hair, breathing hard, she sits at the edge of the bed with clenched jaws, face raised as she struggles with herself. He stands there watching her, refusing to crumble before her need, struggling to keep from rushing in again to assuage her pain . . . waiting for her, in effect, to break.

Interior: Prisoners' visiting room – Day

FELIX *is just being led in by the guard.*

TOM. Andy? Give us a minute, will ya?

Guard releases FELIX *and waits by the door.* FELIX *stands on the other side of dividing counter, suspiciously glancing at* TOM, *and not without hostility.*

TOM. Now look, Felix, I hope you're not gettin' too discouraged, 'cause I'm gaining on it every day now. It won't be long, you are definitely going to walk out of here, you understand?

No response.

You don't know me, Felix; I have my minuses, but I never let go. Understand me? Never. So I want you to start eating, you hear? And focus your thinking on . . .

FELIX *turns and walks to the door . . .* TOM *feels humiliated, and angry too . . .*

I'll be back in a week or two, okay? I'm going to have news . . . !

FELIX *moves through the door without turning back, the guard taking him from there. With a surge of peaking frustration and determination,* TOM *smashes his hat onto his head and storms out.*

Interior: TOM's *bedroom – Night*

TOM *and* CONNIE *asleep. Phone rings. She is awake at once and immediately furious. She reaches over him to the phone.*

CONNIE (*into phone*). . . . . Stop trying to destroy this man, you phoney, you whore!
TOM. Connie! (*He grabs the phone from her. Into phone.*) Listen . . . now wait a minute, I'll come down. Yes, right away. Okay, right, right.

Hangs up. Without a word, gets out of bed and starts dressing.

CONNIE. I can't believe it.
TOM (*angrily and hurriedly throwing on clothes*). I wish you hadn't done that, Connie.
CONNIE. What is happening to you? Tom!
TOM (*white with indignation*). Don't you ever do that again.

CONNIE (*with a plea, now*). What's happening! I don't know you!

TOM. Ever!

The flash of fury in his face silences her. There is a deranged look in his face now. He quickly turns and hurries out of the room.

Interior: McDonald's restaurant, hours later – Night

Except for the two of them and a guy mopping up the place is empty because it is three a.m. and raining outside. He is having a hard time keeping his eyes open, while she is fascinated with herself. Time in large quanties has apparently passed.

ANGELA. . . . So naturally, I got very confused about myself. That's what happens when your father rapes you . . . Am I boring you?

TOM. I didn't say you . . .

ANGELA. Well I beg your fucking pardon!

TOM. It's almost four o'clock in the morning, Angela; at this hour a nudey version of *Gone With The Wind* would put me to sleep.

ANGELA (*touching his hand invitingly*). Come, take me home . . .

TOM. No, tonight I want to talk sitting up.

She indignantly turns away.

– I refuse to believe that for this rendering of your childhood you backed me out of my pyjamas tonight, I just refuse to believe it, kid.

ANGELA. You know what *I'm* beginning to believe? I'm beginning to believe that you are kind of stupid.

TOM. To coin a phrase, honey, by this time I am so confused I couldn't count to twenty-one without taking off my clothes. Did you or didn't you have something to tell me?

ANGELA. I was with John tonight.

TOM. John. – What are you talking about? . . . Callaghan?
Angela? Talk to me . . . *Tonight*?

ANGELA. I love him, Tom. Oh, God, I love him!

TOM. . . . He was really there?

ANGELA (*erupts*). What do you mean, 'really there'!

TOM. What did he want?

ANGELA. His letters back.

It all seems to grind to a halt in TOM. *He is getting silly with
exhaustion.*

TOM. And I suppose you gave them to him and unfortunately
nobody can ever see them again.

ANGELA. No, I didn't give them.

TOM. So you burned them instead, out of bitter disappointment . . . anyway, they're not there any more.

ANGELA. They're there.

TOM. But?

ANGELA (*flaring up*). What am I, a gas station? I have to feel
that we're . . . we're *together*, don't I? – you're asking me
to bomb the love of my life!

He is tempted, and afraid of giving way again.

TOM. All right, okay – I'll take you home, but I'm going to
wait downstairs, and you bring me what you want me to
see. (*Stands.*) Okay?

ANGELA. What are you, afraid of your virginity or something?

TOM. No, I'm afraid of wriggling on the hook again till my
gills dry up. Ready?

ANGELA. In other words, you don't believe one word I've told
you.

TOM. The man's dyin' up there, kid – you got something that
can get him out? – give it to me. (*Lifts her to her feet.*) Let's
go before the sun comes up and blinds us.

ANGELA. I don't like your attitude.

TOM. Neither do I but it's all I got left.

Interior: TOM's *car – Rain – Night*

TOM *is driving through the downpour.* ANGELA *is sitting stiffly, eyes front.*

Close shot: ANGELA: *The terror is rising in her eyes – the passing street lights flash across her breathless gaze.*

ANGELA. I must say, you know, that this kind of mistrust is very annoying.

> *Close shot:* TOM: *He slowly turns to her as he hears the Renata tonality. This is bad news.*

> *She takes out a cigarette – and lights it.*

Exterior: ANGELA's *street – Night*

The car pulls up to her house in the downpour.

Interior: Car – Same time

ANGELA *is sitting very rigidly, smoking 'elegantly'.* TOM *is disarmed, treats her with delicate care, for she is not 'there'.*

TOM. Here we are.

> ANGELA *turns to him, the distant look in her eye. He now dares take her hands in his.*

Please, honey, don't be afraid. I'm with you all the way. (*But he sees she is not moving out.*) . . . Okay, I'll go up with you.

> *He gets out, comes around the car as she is getting out – and notes how demurely she pulls down the hem of her skirt . . .*

Interior: ANGELA's *room – Moments later*

ANGELA *stands there letting* TOM *help her out of her coat. He keeps his on. She stands in thought for a moment, then decides, goes to a book above the filing cabinet and takes a key stashed inside of it. She grasps the padlock . . .*

ANGELA. No, fuck it. I don't have to prove anything – you don't believe me? then go and crack the case by yourself!

TOM. I thought you cared so much about Felix. – Or is there *anything* in there!

ANGELA (*Eleanor Roosevelt*). You are terribly irritating to me!

TOM (*yelling straight to heaven*). What did I do to deserve this!

ANGELA. I must say, what astounds me is how you get to think you're such a high-grade cultured individual and such a great Catholic . . .

TOM. All right, Renata, forget the whole thing . . . !

ANGELA. But all you really are is gutteral!

TOM (*can't help laughing*). You're not even using that word right!

ANGELA. Your whole manner is gutteral because your whole background is gutteral!

TOM (*spreading out his arm*). Okay, Renata, pull out the nails, I want to come down!

ANGELA. *You* can call me Miss Sherwood – stupid bastard.

She sits on the bed, her breath beginning to fail.

TOM. By this time Miss Renata Sherwood ought to know that respectable ladies like her don't call people stupid bastards.

She is dropping back slowly onto the pillow.

ANGELA. Which I would be delighted to do if these stupid bastards had the mental competence to understand any other kind of language, you dumb shit.

ANGELA's eyes are closing and she is breathing deeply. He looks down at her; the key is now becoming visible as her fingers begin to open. He reaches down . . . her fist instinctively clamps shut and she rolls over onto her stomach burying her hand beneath her.

Interior: Diner – Night

Filling up with self-contempt and remorse and guilt, TOM stares at his cup. One or two night-owls sit grinding the night away nearby. He goes to a wall phone, dials.

TOM. Sorry to wake you, Connie, but . . . please, let me talk for a second? I want to apologize. For everything. It all turned out nothing, and I'm a damned fool. Try to forgive me, will you? . . . Who? When! Jesus!

Hangs up and rushes out.

Exterior: Abandoned mill, river – Night

Moving very fast, TOM's car pulls up a distance from the mill, he gets out and goes to a door which is standing ajar.

TOM. Jerry? It's Tom, can I see you?

No response. He enters the place. In the enormous space he can hardly make out anything definite.

Jerry?

He moves to the river side of the building, seeing a large loading door open to the river. He looks outside.

At the very edge of the ramp JERRY is sitting on his motorcycle, its motor idling, front wheel an inch from the drop down. TOM approaches him cautiously, sensing a sort of rapture upon him.

TOM. Hiya.

JERRY seems not to have heard.

Jerry?

JERRY stirs out of his deep reverie.

You called? I just got the message. (*Indicates ignition key.*) Want to shut it off?

TOM *turns the key.*

JERRY. You believe He walked on the water?

TOM. I don't know how to believe it, kid, but I guess there's no way not to – for one of *us*, right?

JERRY *looks out on the dark river flowing by.*

JERRY. You came just in time.

TOM *alerts to this suicide implication, glancing at the river and back to him. He waits, trying to read* JERRY *who, after a moment, dismounts and walks into the mill.*

Interior: Mill – Night

As TOM *follows him in,* JERRY *pulls an electric switch; a ten-foot-high cross lights up, the Major's statute on an improvised box in front of it, and the sacrificial lamb standing in its pen. There are two or three planks on cement blocks as pews. The place, in contrast to the earlier visit, is immaculate.*

TOM. Man, what'd you do here! It's beautiful! You got yourself a church! People coming yet?

JERRY *sits, despair all over him.* TOM *sits near him, trying to decipher him.*

JERRY. I am unclean.

TOM. Truthfully, kid . . . I been kind of wondering about that myself.

JERRY *looks at him.*

You know the saying – coke is high and smack is higher but there's no high on God's earth like a true confession. I respect the agony, kid.

JERRY *stares ahead at* TOM's *meaning, seems to expand toward some beckoning liberation.*

Wanted to say this to you . . . I've talked over the situation with an old friend of mine – without mentioning names. Retired federal judge, used to be one of the great criminal lawyers, smart as a whip. If you'd give him an affidavit, Jer, that you tried to confess about Dr Daniels to the cops that night but they threw you out on the street . . . he's sure the Feds would let you walk – for helpin' them clean out City Hall, y'know? Because the town's gotten horrendous, Jer . . . you know that.

JERRY *looks at him wide-eyed.*

You got a whole life ahead of you, kid. You got something important to say to people! You're a man who *made it*! You understand me? *You made it, Jerry!* Now take what you made.

JERRY *slowly stands.* TOM *stands.* JERRY *turns to him and opens his arms and they embrace . . .*

I'll stick with you, kid, I'll . . .

JERRY. Angie . . . know about this?

TOM. . . . Me coming here? No. Why?

JERRY (*shakes his head remorsefully, but he is excited by his coming rebirth . . . keeps holding onto* TOM's *hand*). See, I kept trying to just talk to him about the new building for my church, but he wouldn't let me in, wouldn't even open the goddamned door. So . . . she . . . I . . . (*Breaks off.*)

TOM. I'm not readin' you, Jer . . .

JERRY. Well, he'd always open up for *her*.

A stillness begins to flow over TOM's *face.*

TOM. Angela . . . was with you?

JERRY. Just so he'd open up . . . see, I wasn't intending to do anything, I swear!

TOM. Right. – So what'd you do, wait in the bushes till he opened the door, . . . or what?

JERRY *nods.*

. . . She didn't go into the house with you, did she?

JERRY. I think so, I don't remember, I just lost my . . . [mind . . .]

TOM (*he can't bear any more*). Okay, let's go! I've got my car . . .

JERRY. No, I want my bike! (*As he backs for the open loading door and his bike, a lofted look on his face . . .*) Y'know? I'm already feeling good about this . . . I *feel* it . . . !

TOM. Oh, you're going to be a new man, Jerry!

TOM, *unable to continue, turns and hurries out the opposite direction – the front door.*

Exterior: Car – Night

The moment TOM *is alone in his car he covers his face and loudly groans in open agony . . .*

The roar of the bike near him – he starts to drive with a cheerful wave to JERRY, *offscreen.*

Exterior: Highway – Night

TOM's *car enters a highway with the bike following several lengths behind.*

Long shot through rear-view mirror of TOM's *car: The bike's single lamp, following steadily. Now it gains on the car, the lamp enlarging in the mirror.*

Exterior: Highway – Same time

JERRY *has sped up alongside* TOM's *window, and, keeping abreast, raises a victorious fist – as though they were now comrades – showing a look of high resolve and happy inner peace.*

TOM *returns the closed-fisted gesture, and* JERRY *drops back to follow the car again.*

Interior: TOM's *car – Same time*

TOM *loses the happy victory grin, and his jaw sets to his formidable task, to get* JERRY's *confession . . . and then to deal with* ANGELA. *He glances up at the mirror and a new flare of anxiety leaps into his face.*

TOM's *point of view: Its headlamp is following steadily, but now* JERRY's *motorcycle speeds up and gains on the car.*

Exterior: Highway – Same time

JERRY, *once again alongside the car, turns to* TOM *with a victoriously raised fist; his expression seems inspired, 'high', and he now roars past in a burst of speed and twenty yards ahead he lifts his hands off the handlebars as though letting a spirit guide him.*

Interior: TOM's *car – Same time*

TOM's *expression is changing from a comradely happiness and amusement to apprehension, and now horror . . .*

Exterior: Highway – Same time

The bike – or rather its headlight and red tail-light and a dimly-seen rider – is out of control and flying off the road . . . into a flaming crash.

Interior: TOM's *kitchen – Day*

TOM *is in his overcoat and hat, and is removing the lid of a cookie jar and then a small pistol.* CONNIE *turns from the sink where she is doing the breakfast dishes as he slips the pistol into his pocket . . .*

TOM. I've got to finish it.
CONNIE. I know.

He starts out.

Just don't buy her nightmares.
TOM. There's still an innocent man in jail.
CONNIE (*absolutely barren of comment*). I know.

He leaves.

Exterior: Woods – Day

TOM *and* MARKS *are walking in silence;* TOM *is glancing at* MARKS, *awaiting his word. They come to a rough bench,* MARKS *sits, then* TOM.

TOM. I really hate taking up your time like this, Harry . . .
MARKS. Forget it; old guys have more time than anything else. – Now tell me the primary question.
TOM. Well . . . she's an accessory to a homicide, correct?
MARKS. Yes. But the witnesses are all kaput.
TOM. Right. But if I could get her to sign a statement that she saw Jerry killing Dr Daniels – You suppose a deal could be cut? – in exchange for her testimony could Felix get a new trial?
MARKS. Listen . . . if she got Abe Daniels to open his door for that killer . . . that's serious business. – Why should she ask for trouble, coming out with that now?
TOM. She's got the monkey on her back. She's eyewitness proof that Felix is innocent. I think this could be what's been making her crazy.
MARKS. Yeah?
TOM. What don't you believe?
MARKS. Well . . . let's spitball. Supposing she did more than

get Jerry into the house; what if she . . . helped him kill the doctor?

TOM. Wow.

MARKS. Who knows what could pop out of the underbrush – there's no end to a woman like this . . . Now listen to me, Tom: I've been traveling the world since my wife died . . . I've lectured in a number of countries on criminal law. Russia, Israel, England, France etcetera. They're all different – except for one thing – corruption. That's everywhere and forever. And kid, winning this case is not going to end it here.

TOM. But Felix is innocent, Harry; I can't get past that. What do you think, is there a possible deal so she doesn't go to jail if she unloads?

MARKS. You're really not going to give up on this . . .

TOM. . . . I can't. Listen . . . (*Grins in embarrassment.*) Can I beg you to give her half an hour? Just to see if there's some angle? I'm desperate for your impression, Harry, I really am.

MARKS. Half an hour. But make it clear to her that I am absolutely not getting involved in this!

TOM. Absolutely not – fantastic!

Interior: Seaside restaurant – Dusk

It is a fish restaurant, quite middle-class, almost empty now, out of season. A view of the ocean from the table. ANGELA *is digging into a lobster.* TOM *studies the drink in front of him.*

TOM. Angela . . .

She glances up at him, with a butter-smudged smile.

We are in a situation.

ANGELA. What situation?

TOM. I was with Jerry just before he died. (*Slight pause.*) He

told me what went down the night he did it to Daniels.
You're an accessory to a homicide.

ANGELA. I'd love a B-and-B.

He summons a waiter.

TOM (*to waiter*). B-and-B for the lady.

The waiter leaves. Another slight pause.

This was what you were trying to cough up, wasn't it . . .
from day one.

ANGELA. I'd love to go dancing, you want to?

TOM. Did you ever confess it to that priest? – No, huh? (*Her
silence concedes this.*) Listen – I have a friend, a retired
federal judge. Used to be one of the great criminal
lawyers . . .

TOM *waits as the waiter sets a B-and-B in front of* ANGELA *and
leaves.*

He'd be willing to see you, Ange.

ANGELA. Why should I see him?

TOM. You're eyewitness testimony that Jerry was at the scene
a few minutes before he was running all over the neighborhood, covered with blood. It just about clears Felix.

ANGELA. And what happens to me?

TOM. That's why I think you ought to talk to the judge.

ANGELA. I want to go somewhere.

TOM. We are somewhere.

ANGELA *moves to get up.*

Please, Ange . . . it's not going to go 'way.

ANGELA (*with a brand new realization*). Why isn't it?

She sees TOM's *eyes – filled with pity for her, but also a certain
direction, and she hears the fearful absence of a reply from
him; he reaches toward her with a calming hand, and with*

new alarm and anger and confusion she flings him off and walks. He quickly leaps up and follows, worried and scared.

Exterior: Boardwalk – Same time

An all-but-deserted resort, with boarded-up rides and ice cream stands, a small Coney Island off-season. They are walking separately, not touching; she emotionally trying to escape, he persistently hanging on. They hear a distant barking and halt, turned toward the sea.

ANGELA. Dogs out there? – They sound hurt.
TOM. No, that's seals, I think. Talking to each other.

They sit on a bench, still not touching.

ANGELA (*a tense attempt at a grin*). You going to turn me in?
TOM. Angela, my evidence died on a motorcycle. How could I turn you in even if I wanted to?
ANGELA (*impatiently now*). What's happening, Tom?
TOM. I think if you dictated a deposition, stating that you got Abe to open the door for Jerry . . .
ANGELA. . . . I'd be accessory to a murder.
TOM. Not necessarily – I mean if Jerry forced you into doing it, it was under duress . . . or if he tricked you. See, this is why I want you to get with the judge.
ANGELA. And what do I do when the rest of it starts coming into it?

TOM goes silent, stalemated.

How does the great Dr Daniels come to've known bums like Jerry and Montana? That has to go straight to the drugs, baby, and that means the cops come into it, right? And then Angela's floatin' out there, feeding those seals.

TOM concedes, lowers his eyes.

TOM. Why did you call me in on this case, Angela?

ANGELA. . . . To spring Felix. I thought maybe you could find some way . . .

TOM. . . . Without involving you. (*She concedes in silence.*) You couldn't bear carrying this any more, is that it?

She barely nods, eyes lowered.

Funny – I keep trying to figure what it is that always pulls me back to you. – It's your conscience. Which nobody is going to believe, but here it is.

This statement of his respect for her pushes a sob into ANGELA, *but it may also be guilt for lying to him. She suddenly strides away down the boardwalk, her conflict intolerable. He hurries after her.*

TOM. Honey! Wait! Angela! Listen to me!

He catches up with her, and she is openly weeping.

ANGELA. Please don't turn me in!

TOM, *wracked, folds her into his arms, but no reassurance comes to his lips.*

Interior: Motel room – Night

TOM, ANGELA. *A 'MOTEL' sign is blinking outside their window. They sit facing each other on two beds. They are still in their coats.*

She is staring, avoiding his eyes. For a long moment nothing is said.

ANGELA. The thing is . . . I don't know if I have enough control; if I ever got on a witness-stand God knows what I might start saying.

TOM. Like what, honey?

ANGELA. Well like . . . I might have made all that up about Callaghan. (*She looks directly at him for the first time.*) . . . I mean I'm not absolutely sure.

TOM (*the question rises in his face – is she slyly using her illness to manipulate him? Or is she really trying to avoid a catastrophe for them both in a court?*). No kidding.

ANGELA. I don't know. I'm almost sure of it, but suddenly every once in a while I . . . (*She breaks off, staring.*)

TOM. But you remember going to the doctor's house that night with Jerry.

ANGELA (*she stares, trying to visualize, then . . .*). I'm not . . . I'm not sure. I'm not even sure Abe Daniels was into drugs.

TOM (*a new hardening, a skepticism, but he downs it*). No kidding.

ANGELA. I couldn't get up on a stand and face John Callaghan. I mean God knows, maybe all I ever did with him was shake hands once in the courthouse. How can I talk to this judge now, you see what I mean? I'm just not sure enough of anything.

TOM *grabs her arm.*

TOM. Honey, there's a few things I know independently of you. – I talked to Jerry myself.

ANGELA (*the faintest hardening*). Jerry was crazier than me. He was brain-damaged. You know, he tried to kill himself –

TOM. Because he'd murdered Daniels. (*Gripping her shoulders, his frustration boiling up in him.*) Hacked his head off, right? (*Shouting close at her.*) Chopped it off? Nearly cut his heart out of his chest?

She tries to draw away but he grips her.

Nobody dreamed *that*, kid.

She is trying to wrench free.

You saw it all, didn't you! Went inside with him, didn't you? Is that it? – You saw him cut his head off, is that what's driving you crazy?

She violently disengages and this makes him sense there is more that she knows, and he rushes to the door and yanks her back into the room.

What'd you, help hold him down, is that it? You held Daniels down for him? Angela!!

A most pleasurable, wild grin grows on her face.

What're you laughing at? (*Shaking her violently.*) Stop laughing at me!

ANGELA. You realize what you're saying to me? You hear your own words? (*Suddenly screaming into his face.*) I helped cut a man's head off? Do you hear your mouth!

He is stunned by the sudden insanity of the idea, for her indignation is very real.

Maybe now you get the feeling – do you? – that everything is possible, and impossible at the same time, right? You feel it? This is what I live with.

With an anguished laugh compounded of contempt and her feeling of loss, she walks out of the room.

Its door opens onto a parking space where his car stands. She walks past it.

Alone for a moment, TOM *is at crisis: what to believe? He rushes out of the room.*

Exterior: Boardwalk – Night

TOM, ANGELA. *She is walking without purpose or destination: her terror is that he may in the end turn her in. She hears him hurrying up to her from behind, and turns in absolute uncertainty to face him again.*

TOM. Okay! Honey, listen: I understand. Let me take you to the judge, see if he can come up with an idea. Just give it a try! (*He takes her hand, pleading.*) He's really one of the greats. I love you, darlin'; I can't help it, I always will.

His unguarded confession seems to move her . . .

ANGELA. . . . If you let me see him alone . . .

TOM (*slightest tinge of suspicion over her relief and joy*). Of course, absolutely!

He takes her hand to move her back to the car, but she turns him back to her. In her face is a sweep of an almost worshipful feeling for him, and a hope of her own resurrection. It is also her instinctive means of control. She grasps his hand and leads him quickly to the sand . . .

TOM (*laughing*). Wait! Listen . . . !

She is pulling him down to the sand, unbuttoning his shirt, biting into his belly . . . a desperation in her fierce, cat-like love-making.

Interior: TOM's car – Later

Driving, sexual contentment on his face, he glances over to her and worry moves into his eyes.

Shot widens to include her; her anxiety is back, but even more tensely as they near the destination.

He pats her thigh reassuringly.

Interior: JUDGE MARK's house – Later

TOM *and* ANGELA *stand before the impressive door to* JUDGE MARKS' *study.* ANGELA *pats her hair, worriedly.*

ANGELA. How . . . how do I look?

TOM. Marvelous. Beautiful.

The door opens. Shooting between TOM'S *and* ANGELA'S *heads we see the surprised excitement on* MARKS' *face as he sees* ANGELA. *Whether it be the shock of her sexuality or her fable, as* TOM *has told it to him, his ageing face lights up with pleasure.*

MARKS. Well! How do you do?

They enter his study.

TOM. I'll take off now, Harry. Be in touch. And I don't have to say how thankful I am. 'Bye, Angela.

She has been absorbing MARKS' *personality, and for an instant doesn't register* TOM'S *farewell, then suddenly turns to him as to an afterthought.*

ANGELA. Oh! – 'Bye.

He senses something like a dismissal, and goes to the door. There he turns for a last farewell.

TOM. Good night, Judge.

MARKS, *his eyes locked on* ANGELA, *waves him off.*

Interior: Coffee shop – Next day

TOM *is nursing a cup, looking at his watch, jiggling a foot on the stool rung. He goes to the wall payphone and dials.*

TOM. Judge Marks' secretary, please. Hi, Jean! – it's me again, has he come in yet? (*As restrained as he can get.*) – Jean, dear, the housekeeper says he's at his office – you wouldn't be kidding ol' Tom, would you? (*Angering.*) Just tell me if he's there so I can stop wasting my time, darlin'. Okay, don't get mad, I believe you.

He hangs up, mystified for a moment, then dials another number.

Connie? Listen, did she call since I left? 'She'? 'She' is Angela Crispini! I think she's avoiding me for some reason; I can't figure it out!

Exterior: ANGELA's *front door – Day*

TOM *is leaning on the buzzer. No answer. Goes around the house to try to see up into her apartment windows. His face is stuffed with mystification and alarm . . . and anger. And perfectly senselessly he yells up . . .*

TOM. Angela!!

Interior: MARKS' *outer office – Shortly after*

JEAN, JUDGE MARKS's *powerhouse secretary is just emerging through a closing door, and* TOM *stands to meet her.*

JEAN. Now listen, Tom, he simply can't be disturbed . . . he's in an important meeting in chambers.
TOM. Jean, please – I'm desperate to find out how it went with a woman I asked him to see.
JEAN. If it's the Epstein case . . .
TOM. That's it, yes . . .
JEAN. Well, he's on his way down from the prison.
TOM. Who's on his way?
JEAN. Felix Epstein. The judge is getting him a new trial. You'll have to excuse me . . .

She goes back through the door she came out of. TOM, *in near shock, lets out a victory laugh, claps his hands together and rushes off, astounding several passing lawyer types in the corridor.*

Exterior: Courthouse – Day

At the peak of anxiety and happiness, TOM *is hurrying to a public phonebooth at the entrance of the courthouse. As he dials, a hostile cop walks by, giving him a dour look which* TOM *returns with a wink and a pistol-mime with his forefinger. Into phone . . .*

TOM. Connie! I did it! Epstein is out! The judge hasn't called, has he? – I don't know, the secretary says he's getting him a new trial . . . *(Seeing something off-camera.)* Hey! Call you back!

Exterior: Courthouse area – Day

TOM'*s viewpoint.* MARKS *is on the sidewalk below the courthouse steps, walking toward a limousine parked at the curb.*

Exterior: Courthouse area – Day

TOM *is rushing down the steps . . .*

TOM. Judge! Wait!

Exterior: Courthouse area – Day

TOM *rushes up to* MARKS, *who turns to him, but with an inexplicable air of reserve . . .*

TOM. My God, Harry – Jean just told me you got him out! She must really have impressed you, huh? – Angela?
MARKS. Remarkable woman.

MARKS *turns and moves to the limo whose driver is opening the door for him.* TOM, *mystified, follows him . . .*

TOM. Harry . . . what's wrong? You mad at me or something?

MARKS. This is a very deep woman, a sensitive woman. You had no call being that rough on her.

TOM (*flummoxed*). Me! How was I rough?

MARKS. You either believe her or you don't, there's no need to be hounding her.

TOM. Harry, please! I was only trying to get her to tell what she knows. (*Flattering.*) But I knew she'd agree to testify the minute you got your hands on her!

MARKS (*stalwart protectiveness*). No, no! There's no need for her to enter the court. – Callaghan failed to reveal exculpatory evidence to the defense – it's a technicality, but enough to reverse.

Alarm springs onto TOM'S *face as* MARKS *starts to bend to get into the car.* TOM *dares to grasp his arm in his desperation.*

TOM. Harry, please listen – there's a whole connection to the police that she knows about. The case is all about drugs and Callaghan and the police department – it goes to the top of the mountain!

MARKS. No-no, Epstein will be a free man and that's the end of it . . .

TOM. But she could expose the corruption of the whole state, she could hang them all out to dry!

MARKS. Now listen to me! The killer is dead. And the poor woman has been through enough! That's the end of it!

MARKS *bends and enters the car and the chauffeur shuts the door behind him, and gets behind the wheel.* TOM *can't help one more try and bends to speak to the judge through the closed window . . .*

TOM. Harry . . . I can't believe this!

He sees something within the car that splashes his face with astonishment.

TOM's *point of view:* ANGELA *in the back seat is lifting a tentative finger of greeting to* TOM *as* MARKS *stares at her with stars in his eyes. The car pulls away.*

Exterior: Limo back window – Same time

TOM's *view point:* ANGELA *has turned around, and looking out the rear window of the limo at* TOM, *is lifting both hands and squinching up her shoulders, happily declaring her helplessness before her victory, as well as begging his understanding of her happy plight. She blows him a kiss. Two, in fact.*

Exterior: Street – Day

He is open-mouthed watching the car moving away.

Dissolve. Now a serio-comical kind of orchestration blots out the sound of the following: over the above a small crowd on courthouse steps: TV crews in action, interviewing FELIX, *who is now shaved and looking pretty good in a business suit, with a topcoat over his arm, and* ANGELA *beside him, looking terrific:*

FELIX. I owe everything to this wonderful woman! Thanks, Angela!

And beside her stands JUDGE MARKS *grasping her elbow as he speaks into an interviewer's microphone.*

While next to him stands JOHN CALLAGHAN *manifestly agreeing with what he is telling the TV interviewer, namely . . .*

MARKS. No-no, there are no hard feelings with my old friend John Callaghan. An honest mistake was made and it is now rectified. I must say, though, that only the noble efforts of this remarkable woman have righted this terrible injustice to an innocent man!

ANGELA (*smack into the lens*). What can I say? I want to thank the judge and . . . I don't know, just to be able to look at this man (FELIX, *that is.*), standing at last in the open sunshine like this, gives me such a feeling of happiness that I can only say thank you, thank you, thank you . . . !

While she is thanking everybody, the music thunders out of her and the camera sweeps across the crowd in the midst of which in a

Close shot: TOM *and* CONNIE

we find the couple looking on, and in a momentary lull in the volume of the music . . .

CONNIE. It's really remarkable – everybody wins!
TOM (*with a deep, ironic nod*). . . . Almost.

Camera swiftly rises over the crowd, the courthouse, the town . . .

Methuen World Classics

Aeschylus (two volumes)
Jean Anouilh
John Arden (two volumes)
Arden & D'Arcy
Aristophanes (two volumes)
Aristophanes & Menander
Peter Barnes (two volumes)
Brendan Behan
Aphra Behn
Edward Bond (four volumes)
Bertolt Brecht
    (four volumes)
Howard Brenton
    (two volumes)
Büchner
Bulgakov
Calderón
Anton Chekhov
Caryl Churchill
    (two volumes)
Noël Coward (five volumes)
Sarah Daniels (two volumes)
Eduardo De Filippo
David Edgar (three volumes)
Euripides (three volumes)
Dario Fo (two volumes)
Michael Frayn (two volumes)
Max Frisch
Gorky
Harley Granville Barker
    (two volumes)
Henrik Ibsen (six volumes)

Terry Johnson
Lorca (three volumes)
David Mamet
Marivaux
Mustapha Matura
David Mercer (two volumes)
Arthur Miller
    (five volumes)
Anthony Minghella
Molière
Tom Murphy
    (three volumes)
Musset
Peter Nichols (two volumes)
Clifford Odets
Joe Orton
Louise Page
A. W. Pinero
Luigi Pirandello
Stephen Poliakoff
    (two volumes)
Terence Rattigan
Ntozake Shange
Sophocles (two volumes)
Wole Soyinka
David Storey (two volumes)
August Strindberg
    (three volumes)
J. M. Synge
Ramón del Valle-Inclán
Frank Wedekind
Oscar Wilde

Methuen Modern Plays

include work by

Jean Anouilh
John Arden
Margaretta D'Arcy
Peter Barnes
Brendan Behan
Edward Bond
Bertolt Brecht
Howard Brenton
Simon Burke
Jim Cartwright
Caryl Churchill
Noël Coward
Sarah Daniels
Nick Dear
Shelagh Delaney
David Edgar
Dario Fo
Michael Frayn
Paul Godfrey
John Guare
Peter Handke
Jonathan Harvey
Declan Hughes
Terry Johnson
Barrie Keeffe
Stephen Lowe

Doug Lucie
John McGrath
David Mamet
Patrick Marber
Arthur Miller
Mtwa, Ngema & Simon
Tom Murphy
Peter Nichols
Joseph O'Connor
Joe Orton
Louise Page
Luigi Pirandello
Stephen Poliakoff
Franca Rame
Philip Ridley
David Rudkin
Willy Russell
Jean-Paul Sartre
Sam Shepard
Wole Soyinka
C. P. Taylor
Theatre de Complicite
Theatre Workshop
Sue Townsend
Timberlake Wertenbaker
Victoria Wood